A GARDEN STYLE B

HOMEGROWN FRUIT

[SIMPLE SECRETS FOR GLORIOUS GARDENS—INDOORS AND OUT]

MIMI LUEBBERMANN

PHOTOGRAPHY BY FAITH ECHTERMEYER

CHRONICLE BOOKS

SAN FRANCISCO

Library of Congress Cataloging-in-Publication Data:
Luebbermann, Mimi.
Homegrown fruit: simple secrets for glorious
gardens, indoors and out / by Mimi Luebbermann:
photographs by Faith Echtermeyer.
            p.   cm.
"A Garden Style Book."
Includes bibliographical references (p. 106) and index.
ISBN 0-8118-1602-8 (pb)
1. Fruit-culture. 2. Fruit. I. Title.
SB355.L835 1998
634—dc21   97-30799
                        CIP

Printed in Hong Kong

Cover and interior design by
Aufuldish & Warinner

Distributed in Canada by Raincoast Books,
8680 Cambie Street, Vancouver, B.C. V6P 6M9

10 9 8 7 6 5 4 3 2 1

Chronicle Books
85 Second Street
San Francisco, CA 94105

Web Site: www.chronbooks.com

Contents

POTTED FRUIT   45

VINES AND BRAMBLES   55

FRUITING SHRUBS   67

FRUIT TREES 75

HEIRLOOM AND EXOTIC VARIETIES 85

INTO THE KITCHEN 97

Introduction

Fruit, fabulous fruit: juice dripping down your chin from a peach so ripe that a dozen napkins can hardly contain its sweetness. The crunch of a tree-ripened apple that only moments before was snapped off the fruiting spur. The fragrant burst of a grape under your teeth; the crisp, clean taste of lemons; the puckery nip of gooseberries—all these define fruitfulness.

¶No garden is too small to grow fruit, even if you have space only for containers on a fire escape or balcony, or a tiny back garden. Strawberries can hang over the edge of a window box, citrus will bloom fragrantly in tubs, and grafted dwarf trees can produce three or more different varieties of fruit in a flower bed. Clever gardeners espalier fruit trees flat against house or garage walls. Dwarf fruit trees trained along wire trellises create a low hedge that flowers in spring and fruits in summer. Berries clothe an ugly fence, and grapes climb languorously up trellises to droop heavy fruit clusters.

¶When we bite into a homegrown fruit, we discover fresh-picked flavor *that has no parallel in the marketplace. Ripened to a point of perfection on the shrub, tree, or vine, fruit explodes with flavor.*

¶In growing your own fruit, you will join in an age-old tradition. Humans have been growing fruit as long as they have farmed. Tribes migrating across Europe transported little wild apples that originated in Eastern Europe and Asia. In Mesopotamia, where nomads first settled down to become farmers, they grew figs, dates, and grapes, along with wheat.

¶In succeeding centuries, orchards were included in enclosed gardens where the Persians grew flowers, trees, and crops protected from hungry animals. According to Penelope Hobhouse, in Gardening Through the Ages, *by* A.D. *1050, almonds, apples, apricots, bananas, brambles, cherries, figs, grapes, jujubes, mulberries, olives, oranges, and plums were widely grown, and Egyptian art from the time of the pharaohs illustrates grapes, mulberries, and figs.*

¶Although the Greeks first began to graft and experiment with improving fruit types, it was during the Roman conquest and the long tranquil period of that empire that the most important steps in fruit-tree development took place. The Romans used grafting and budding techniques to improve the quality of fruit. As Roman troops flowed over Europe, they spread their horticultural advancements. When the Roman Empire collapsed, most of the horticultural knowledge and the plants themselves disappeared, except for those maintained in monasteries. During medieval times, fruit crops again multiplied and the old skills were renewed. By the seventeenth century, the art of grafting was common knowledge and grafted trees were preferred over the unpredictable sports, or mutations, resulting from seeds, although for colonists setting out to far-off countries, seeds were often more practical to carry regardless of the results.

¶During the European exploration of the New World in the sixteenth and seventeenth centuries, exotic plants were imported to Europe, making new fruits available. Heated glass houses, called orangeries, protected tropical fruits, mostly citrus, in the coldest of climates. With the invention of industrially produced

sheet glass, greenhouses became common among the new middle class, and gardening became the purview of the common people. Everyone who could afford it wanted a fruit garden, and plants became widely available due to increased demand.

¶The newly discovered continent of North America became a crossroads of fruit brought in from all over the world. Its geographic and climatic diversity allowed Americans to grow almost every fruit found on the planet. The Native Americans tutored the colonialists in the edible fruits in the new land, and the settlers began hybridizing wild trees with cultivated fruit trees from Europe. All kinds of fruit came to America brought by settlers from Spain, France, and England, so that melons, figs, dates, pineapples, citrus, and bananas, to name a few, could be found growing in a location with an amenable climate.

¶Later, that tireless apple missionary Johnny Appleseed, whose real name was Jonathan Chapman, spread apple trees by planting seeds as well as by giving them away. Pocketing free seeds he collected from pomace, the crushed apple pulp left over from pressing cider, he traveled through the wilderness planting seeds. By the time he died in 1847, he had planted trees in 100,000 square miles of Ohio and Indiana.

¶In those days, long before supermarkets, everyone had an orchard, but as urban centers began to grow in response to the Industrial Revolution in the second half of the nineteenth century, market gardeners clustered outside large cities. They grew a variety of fruits and vegetables, which they delivered to city residents in horse carts or at farmers' markets, or sold to greengrocers who serviced households and businesses. The fruits, tailored to a specific climate and harvested successively through the growing seasons, offered a tremendous variety of seasonal, regional produce.

¶In the twentieth century, with the advent of refrigerated railroad cars, the produce industry changed. Now, fruits could be picked green and shipped from local venues to regional and national markets. New Yorkers relished tropical fruits, and Floridians shopped in the markets for cherries and apples impossible to grow in their climate. By the middle of the century, air freight began to bring in international produce, so *fresh strawberries in November and watermelon in January became the norm in every supermarket.*

¶There was a price for such extravagant flaunting of the seasons. Regional fruits, which needed to be fully ripened for the best flavor, began to disappear because they bruised in shipping and didn't keep long enough on store shelves. Fruits were picked green and left in cold storage for months and months. When ripe fruit was needed, fruit was taken to warmer rooms and exposed to ethylene gas, which caused them to ripen. Those who had never tasted a fully ripe fruit accepted the mealy, pallid-tasting substitute as the real thing.

¶As a result, of the seven thousand varieties of apples available today, only three or four commercially reliable types can generally be found in stores. Apricots with names like Alexis, Harris, St. Ambroise, and Montgamet disappeared, and a fruit called only "apricot" appeared in stores, as if there were only one type.

¶Gardeners who have continued to grow their own fruit, however, know the intense flavor of homegrown fruit. Often, they grow heirloom varieties, old-fashioned plants and trees that suit their local climates and bear fruit reliably with a fragrance and texture unlike the tasteless products sold in markets. With the current resurgence of interest in fine-flavored fruits, the old-fashioned varieties, never seen in stores, are now more widely available through catalogues. Many of these types have been meticulously rescued from extinction by collectors who hunted ramshackle home sites, weedy graveyards, and deserted orchards for old varieties whose scions, or small branches, grafted to new rootstock and carefully nurtured, produced fruits that had been thought lost. Today, their efforts are a boon to every backyard gardener.

¶Growing fruit puts you in touch with the flow of the seasons. As winter gradually fades, spring blossoms delicately perfume the air, and nubs of fruit gradually swell to maturity. Soon fruit overflows baskets and buckets, an embarrassment of riches to eat out of hand, to inspire new creations in the kitchen, to put up into jellies and preserves, and to give to grateful friends. Fall brings colored leaves, gradually drifting into patches of color on the ground. Even though you may live in a city with a restricted gardening space, you can savor every gift of growing fruit all through the year.

Characteristics of Fruit

The scrumptious fruit we treasure for flavor and texture, juice and fragrance, is actually, according to the dictionary, the ripened ovary of a seed plant. It seems that nature, in all its wisdom, created fruit simply as an enticing package for a seed.

¶Seeds must sprout far enough away from the mother plant to have room to grow. Some seeds have special mechanisms for dispersal, from the parachutelike fluff that elevates dandelion seeds to distant pastures or neighbors' lawns to the sticky burr or hooked surfaces with which seeds hitch a ride on pant legs or furred bodies. Others developed fruit, another clever method of passive seed distribution. The covering tissue feeds and protects the seed, and as the fruit ripens, the seed matures. The tempting fruit easily beguiles a creature into eating it, thus providing the necessary vehicle to carry it from the source, to be deposited in another location. Mammals are not the only creatures that transfer seeds in their hands, paws, fur, or digestive systems. Lizards, earthworms, snails, tortoises, and birds also partake of fruit and thus spread the seeds.

¶The variation of seed size and shape is astonishing. Sometimes a fruit is filled with seeds, like the passion fruit, papaya, or blackberry. Or there may just be a few pips, as in grapes, or one large seed, as in an avocado or mango. Seeds can stay alive outside a fruit for decades.

¶Many fruits today are hybridized, with complicated parentage, and as a consequence, the seeds do not produce a true duplicate of the parent plant. Gardeners who want to save seeds for replanting must first check the heritage of the plant. Only seeds of open-pollinated, or non-hybridized, plants sprout for a reliable harvest.

FRUIT CATEGORIES

Within the world of plant physiology, categories can contradict a fruit's common name. A blackberry, for example, is classified not as a berry but as an aggregate fruit, while a watermelon is termed a hard-shelled berry. Yet, the general classifications used by fruit growers are simple: orchard, or tree fruits; vine fruits; and shrub fruits. The tree category is divided into stone fruits, citrus, and pomes, a term that includes apples, quinces, and pears. Stone fruits, also known as drupes, bear a single seed that is surrounded by a hard shell and enclosed in a fleshy fruit. Pome fruits have small seeds within a core. The stem around the core swells up to totally enclose the seeds. Both stone fruits and pome fruits are members of the Rosaceae family.

¶Vine fruits include kiwis, grapes, passion fruit, tomatoes, melons, and pumpkins. Strawberries are included in this category, although they are not a true fit. Shrub fruits include berries that grow on branches or canes such as blueberries, gooseberries, and currants.

POLLINATION

Fruit appears only after pollination of the flower. Bees, moths and butterflies, flies, bats, beetles, and the wind all help the pollen, which is produced in the anthers, the male part of a flower, to reach the stigma, the female part of the flower. The pollen travels down the stigma to fertilize the egg cells, triggering the growth of tissue that encases the seed. In some cases, flowers are self-pollinating, or self-fruitful, because they are both male and female. Many fruit trees are self-sterile, meaning they need to be pollinated by another cultivar, or variety, in order to produce fruit. The trees must bloom at the same time to transfer pollen for fertilization, so an early-blooming type matched with a late variety will not prove effective. If space is at a premium, plant a grafted type with four or more different varieties, or consider planting two different trees in the same hole (see page 80).

SIZES OF TREES

The mature size of fruit trees depends on the rootstock. Although some trees are grown from seeds, for an exact clone of the parent a branch of the desired variety—called a scion—is grafted to a rootstock that has been chosen for its vigor, disease resistance, and size. Grafting is the process of bonding the branch of one plant, with all its genetic material, to that of another by root grafting, branch grafting, or bud grafting so that the two different plants grow together. Although the rootstock controls the final size of the tree and may add disease resistance, the grafted material will produce fruit that is true to its parentage.

¶Thanks to grafting, you can choose the same variety of fruit tree in multiple sizes. For example, a Golden Delicious apple can be grown as a dwarf, a mid-sized, or a standard-sized tree. Select the kind of tree that will fit the space you have when it has grown to mature size. If you wish to espalier or prune the tree to a special shape, a dwarf or mid-sized tree works best. For containers, a dwarf tree is preferable. Don't worry that a small tree won't produce as much; figuring the yield per growing area, dwarfs produce *more* than a standard-sized tree.

¶Genetically dwarf trees, which grow naturally smaller than standard-sized trees grown on dwarf rootstock, come in

a wide variety of types, from cherries to peaches and nectarines. These trees are prolific, long-lived, and take up a minimal amount of space. A genetically dwarf tree is exceptionally small because the tree, itself small, is grafted on a dwarf rootstock to further reduce the size.

CHILLING HOURS

Fruit trees require a minimum of "chilling hours," or temperatures below 45°F, per year. The number of chilling hours needed depends on the type of fruit and the specific cultivar. A high chill requirement calls for low winter temperatures, while a low-chill fruit type needs fewer hours of weather below 45°F. Different varieties require varying amounts of prolonged cold weather, without which they will not flower or fruit successfully. Eventually, in a climate consistently warmer than the requirements, the tree weakens and dies. Your local extension agent or neighborhood nursery can tell you the minimum number of chilling hours for your area and recommend trees that match your climate. Even in mild-winter areas like the San Francisco Bay region, there are low-chill cultivars that can succeed regardless of the warm winters.

¶Don't confuse chilling hours, meaning the amount of cold weather needed by a tree in dormancy, with frost tenderness. Trees with low chill requirements, appropriate to mild-winter climates, must still be matched to seasonal frosts, because chilling hours do not indicate frost hardiness. Early-bearing trees—which bloom early—can have buds or blooms injured by frost, damaging crops. Freezing weather or rainy weather just when the flowers emerge can inhibit pollination, causing a poor yield that year. So if your mild-winter climate has a tendency to late spring frosts, select a late-bearing fruit variety to protect your crop.

GROWTH PATTERNS

Deciduous fruit trees grow in two ways: bearing fruit at the tips of the branches or on fruiting spurs, or short lateral branches. Trees like persimmons bear fruit at the tips, or terminals, of their branches, while apples, pears, and plums, among others, send out fruiting spurs that produce flowers and fruit. Branches that grow horizontally tend to produce more fruiting spurs than those that shoot straight up in the air. Although there are generally enough branches on a tip-bearing tree to bear a harvest after pruning, radical pruning of such a tree can cut off most of the yielding wood, consequently diminishing the harvest.

¶Fruit trees set more fruit than they can ripen. When the fruit is about one inch in diameter, there is a natural thinning of excess fruits, so don't be surprised to see a carpet of dropped fruit on the ground. This early summer drop still leaves more fruit on the tree than it may be able to bear, so the gardener must continue to thin by hand. Take off the smallest fruits, or those that appear insect damaged. Thinning secures a harvest of plump, full-sized fruits with intense flavor.

¶Fruit plants such as apricots may be alternate bearing, meaning they fruit heavily one year while the next year's harvest is light, so that although the spring weather may be perfect, the summer crop is quite small. Often, thinning fruits helps trees bear more evenly from year to year.

¶Vines need care to thin out their vigorous growth, bringing light to the fruit and making space for new stems during pruning. They may fruit on new wood or in some cases on old wood. Learn the growing pattern of each specific vine so you can tailor the pruning and thinning of stems to each one.

¶Berries grow by producing a multitude of stems, called canes. Depending on the variety, some throw up a thicket of canes while others grow only a moderate number. Some berries bear biennially; that is, they send up a cane one year and the next year the cane develops buds and fruit. Shrub fruits like blueberries can take up to four years to produce fruit on the branches. Pruning keeps these plants producing a succession of fruit-bearing stems.

Growing fruit

Growing fruit successfully depends on the gardener's attention to the plants' needs. With fruit plants in particular, gardeners must match the garden environment to their requirements, choosing plants that suit the amount of available summer heat and winter chill for a satisfactory harvest. Equally important is maintaining the fertility of the soil and providing adequate water. Pruning to maintain health and increase harvest should be timed to the rhythm of each plant's emergence from dormancy into bloom and fruiting. Understanding how the plants grow makes it easier to tailor an effective maintenance program for specific fruits.

Water

A plant is an efficient mechanism, with all its parts working to provide food and water for its growth and maturation. The roots are like straws, drawing water and nutrients out of the soil into the plant. The water is sucked through the roots and drawn out on to the surface of the leaves, where the sun causes the water to evaporate through their pores. The water evaporating off the surface of the leaves pulls more water through the plant from the roots. The entire process is known as transpiration.

¶During periods of high evaporation from the leaves, such as hot or windy days, the rate of water loss increases, so roots require more water. When the leaves lose more water than the roots can quickly replenish, the plant wilts. This explains why a healthy plant can die from lack of water. Increase your watering when the weather turns sultry or windy, because under these conditions a plant will need more water than usual.

¶Just as plants can die from too little water, they can die from too much. In order to breathe, roots need oxygen, which they find in the spaces between soil particles. Normally, when an area of soil fills with water, gravity pulls the water down through the spaces between the particles, allowing oxygen to fill them again. A heavy clay layer can create a pooling effect, preventing drainage and causing the roots of the plant to rot. Similarly, plants may die if set into a dip or depression where the water puddles during times of heavy rains and stays for periods of days. In both of these situations, simply digging a large planting hole and filling it with amendments does not solve the situation. If a planting hole does not drain within 5 minutes, continue digging down until you break through the clay layer. In a location where water collects, plant the root ball above the soil level, adding soil to cover the root ball and fill in the depression.

FERTILIZERS AND NPK BALANCE

The major nutrients needed for plant growth are nitrogen, phosphorus, and potassium, usually noted by their chemical abbreviations N, P, and K. A plant in the ground removes these nutrients from the soil and uses them to grow stems, leaves, blossoms, and fruit or seeds. Most fruiting plants need a soil rich in nutrients in order to produce fruit. Make sure to fertilize during periods of rapid growth, when a plant's nutrient needs are greatest. Most plants spurt in spring and summer, although there are some exceptions to this rule. Decrease fertilizing during fall and winter to encourage plants into dormancy and prevent new tender growth susceptible to frost.

¶Commercial fertilizers list their contents as the percentage of nitrogen, phosphorus, and potassium. For example, an NPK formula of 10-10-10 has equal amounts of nitrogen, phosphorus, and potassium, while one of 20-20-20 is twice as strong. Potassium and phosphorus stimulate root and bloom growth, while nitrogen feeds foliage growth. All-purpose fertilizers have a balanced formula for maximum growth of roots and good growth of leaves and blooms. Although it may seem that if some fertilizer is good, more must be better, do not overfertilize plants. Like overfeeding people, overfeeding plants can encourage unhealthy excess growth.

¶Manufacturers' claims and scientific studies differ on just how long slow-release fertilizers continue to dissolve and release in the soil, for watering habits, temperature, and the plant's needs all produce different effects. For the best results, add slow-release fertilizer to the soil yearly, either in late fall or in early spring. In late fall, slow-release granules, their release retarded by temperature, will not overfeed the plants but will become available in spring when most needed.

¶Liquid fertilizers can be applied to boost plants that are heavy feeders, particularly just before blooming. Applying diluted formulas every 2 weeks is more effective for plant growth than more intense solutions applied monthly. Check the manufacturer's instructions for the proper dilution, then if applying every 2 weeks, add twice as much water.

¶You may want to consider using organic fertilizers for your homegrown fruit. Although there have been no conclusive studies, there are a number of testimonials to the improved taste of fruit grown using organic fertilizers. Look for the certified-organic slow-release fertilizer granules to add to the soil when planting or yearly in the fall. Or you can add equal parts of blood meal (N), bone meal (P), and wood ashes (K). Try different methods to find one that works best for you. Composted steer manure is another inexpensive organic fertilizer that adds both fiber and nutrition to the soil, although adding too much can damage plants. Applied together with a mulch, steer manure gradually decomposes into the soil. Kelp, cottonseed, and other non-animal organic fertilizers are also widely available.

DRIP LINE/ROOTS

The drip line is an imaginary circle drawn on the ground around the plant at the end of its branches. If it were raining, this circle would indicate the drips from the tips of the plant's branches. The drip line was once thought to be the farthest point the roots extended underground. Research has shown, however, that roots actually extend beyond the drip line of plants, and the older the plants, the farther the roots extend. Feeder roots, the young tender tips of roots located primarily at the edge of the root mass, expand out through the soil absorbing most of the water and nutrition for the plant. Therefore, watering or fertilizing at the trunk of the tree is ineffective, because the water or nutrients don't reach the

feeder roots. Consequently, as plants grow, continue to water and fertilize farther and farther out from the trunk.

SITE

Fruiting plants are affected by both summer heat and winter chill. Some plants require more heat and more cold, while others prefer warmer winters and cooler summers. Plants with growing needs that match the site's climate will be healthier and bear more fruit than plants in less-favorable conditions. Most fruiting plants need at least 4 to 6 hours of sunlight a day, but they can survive with less although yield may be affected. In hot summer climates, plants that require cooler temperatures may need some shade to offset the high temperatures.

¶Your garden is full of microclimates, some just feet away from each other. A sunny south-facing exposure, warm in the winter, has less heat in the summer than a sunny west-facing exposure against a wall, which can produce reflected temperatures over 100°F even on mildly warm days. In cold winter areas, some less-hardy plants may appreciate the extra warmth of a south-facing house wall underneath a roof overhang.

PLANTING

Many fruit plants can be purchased for a limited time in early spring from nurseries and catalogues in bare root, meaning that the plant's roots are exposed without any soil, just encased in plastic with a portion of wood chips or newsprint around them to keep them from drying out. Bare-root plants are more inexpensive than potted ones and a greater variety of them may be offered in both nurseries and catalogues. However, because their roots are exposed, it is critical to get them into the ground quickly.

¶In early spring, the ground may still be too wet for planting. When digging at the start of the season, if the soil clumps and falls off the shovel in large lumps, then the ground is too wet and you must wait to let it dry out a bit more. Working wet soil compacts it, forcing out the oxygen and leaving a rock-hard planting bed. In this case, you need to make a temporary home for the plants, a process called "heeling in," until you can set them in their permanent position.

¶To heel in your plants, dig a trench in a shaded area that stays cool all day. Make sure the trench is just large enough to hold the entire root system of the plants. Cut one side of the trench at a 45-degree angle, and the other straight down. Lay the plants so their roots are in the deepest part of the trench, with the trunk resting on the angled side, and water them well. Replace the soil and water again. Continue to keep the soil moist to prevent the roots from drying out until you can plant. Try to plant within a couple of weeks, or before the plants begin to leaf out. When you are ready to set in your plants, immerse them in a bucket of water for at least 12 to 24 hours to thoroughly soak the roots.

¶The latest research has changed the traditional method of planting. Strong root development leads to healthy plants, and instructions in the past have been to dig a large hole for a new plant. Now, we know from the latest studies that digging a generously sized hole and filling it with compost, soil amendments, and fertilizer actually does a disservice to the plant. The planting hole, with its added superior soil and excellent nutrients, does not encourage the plant to send roots into the generally inferior soil of the surrounding area. Consequently, the roots may simply encircle the hole, as if potbound. Additionally, during rainy weather, sub-surface water can pool up in the looser textured soil of the planting hole, sometimes drowning the plant.

¶Consequently, when planting, dig a hole just large enough to accommodate the existing roots. Mound up a pyramid of soil in the middle of the hole and spread out the roots over it. Return the original soil to the hole, not adding any amendments or fertilizer. As you add the soil, tamp it down firmly, making sure not to leave any air pockets around the roots. When the hole is half refilled with dirt, fill it with water, making sure the plant does not sink below the level of the soil. Gently pulling up on the plant while repacking the soil restores it to the proper height. Continue adding soil until the hole is filled. As an added impetus to encourage the roots to spread out, water or place a drip system out from the trunk beyond the edge of the hole to urge the plant's roots to search for food and water.

¶When setting in, or planting, plants, make sure to keep the soil level just above the roots at the earlier planted level, which you can usually discern by a subtle change of color in the bark just above the root crown. Set in a grafted plant with the graft union at least 2 inches above the soil line and with the graft facing due north, to avoid the sun damage known as sunscald on the sensitive bark.

Setting the plant at the correct level is particularly important for grafted plants to avoid rotting the graft wood, which would allow the rootstock itself to grow into a plant.

¶Mulching plants insulates the ground, conserving moisture and maintaining soil temperatures while preventing the formation of a crust that can inhibit water saturation. Mulch piled up on the trunk or stems, however, can contribute to crown rot, a disease that causes the death of many plants, especially fruit trees. Add mulch when you plant, but pull it 2 inches away from the trunk or stems of the plants. Many gardeners like to spread a slow-release pelleted fertilizer around the drip line of the plants in the fall, then renew the mulch on top of the fertilizer. Spreading the fertilizer out from the stem of the plants encourages the roots to reach out, both improving stabilization and encouraging better nutrition from root growth. The cool night temperatures of fall inhibit a plant from absorbing fertilizer, preventing the tender growth that might be harmed by late frosts.

STARTING FROM SEEDS

Starting your own plants from seeds is easy, and it offers you the advantage of growing a wide range of varieties that nurseries do not regularly stock as small plants. If you live in a cold climate with a short growing season, starting seeds inside produces vigorous plants that are ready for transplanting into outside pots when the weather warms up. Seeds also can be sown directly into their permanent pots later, when the warmth of spring encourages germination and there is no danger of frost. Whether you plan to sow indoors or outdoors, order your seeds for spring and summer sowing in January to make sure you start with fresh high-quality stock. (Some seed sources are listed on page 106.)

¶Check your nursery for the choice of seed-starting kits, such as Styrofoam flats, plastic six-packs, or peat pots. Choose pots or containers with individual sections for each seedling so that the transplants will pop out of them easily.

¶Seeds need temperatures of between 65° and 75°F to germinate. Some gardeners place heat mats underneath germinating trays to keep the soil evenly warm. A sunny south window may provide enough warmth and light. If not, you can hang Gro-lights or full-spectrum lights 4 to 6 inches above the containers. If your plants lean toward the light source and

look skinny and weak, they are not getting enough light.

¶Start your seeds 6 to 8 weeks before you want to put plants outside. It is important to use a sterilized mix to avoid diseases that infect seedlings. To make sure the plants get off to a good start, add half the recommended amount of an all-purpose slow-release fertilizer to the mix according to the manufacturer's directions, or once the seedlings are 1 inch high, water them once a week with a low-nitrogen fertilizer diluted to half strength.

¶Thoroughly moisten the mix with water, then fill the seed container with mix to within 1 inch of the rim. Sow the seeds at the correct depth and spacing according to the recommended directions on the seed packet. After you have sown the seeds, pat down the mix firmly and water carefully using a watering can with a perforated cap so you don't dislodge the seeds. Keep the mix moist but not soggy to avoid encouraging fungal infections. Place the seed containers where they will get 2 to 4 hours of bright sun a day. If the seedlings begin to stretch up, lean over, and look leggy, they are not receiving enough light. When roots begin to show at the bottom of the container, the young plants are

ready to be set out of doors or into larger containers. Don't wait any longer or your plants will become root bound, which can retard their growth.

VITAMIN B1

Although touted for years as the means to lessen transplantation shock to the delicate roots of plants, studies of Vitamin B1 have shown that it is ineffective in encouraging feeder roots to regrow so that the plant can absorb water and nutrients. Although gardeners may feel comforted by its use, it does not speed plant recovery. Keeping a transplanted plant well watered for several days while the feeder roots regrow is the most effective means of speeding the plant's recovery.

PAINTING THE TRUNK

Young fruit trees in nurseries are often grown thickly, as if in miniature forests. In this situation, the trees shade each other, but when you set them out in your garden, like the skin of sunbathers in early summer, their tender bark may suffer sunscald, which can irreparably damage the trunk and leave it susceptible to wood borers. Painting the trunks up to the second branch with interior or exterior

latex—not oil-based—paint protects
them from an injury that has the potential to be fatal. Paint at least 1 inch or
more below the level of the soil by
pulling the soil back, then letting the
paint dry before replacing the soil.

SPACING

Gardeners often have a problem visualiz-
ing a thin, skinny stick transforming itself
into a stately 30-foot-high tree within a
short five or six years. A little kiwi vine,
scarcely climbing out of a 1-gallon container, can within a few years stretch out
to cover 20 to 30 feet of trellis. Not antici-
pating the size a plant grows to can create
a space problem necessitating extensive
pruning that may limit the harvest. If you
need a companion tree as a pollinator, the
result may be overcrowding.

¶ Overly crowding plants inhibits air circulation, creating a climate for disease.
Also, soil fertility can be drained by the
demands of too many plants in too small
an area. Both these problems can be
solved, or at least addressed, by paying
attention to spacing. Rules can be broken, as long as the grower anticipates and
plans to overcome the problems. Twenty-
foot-tall hedges of standard fruit trees can
be kept under control with careful pruning

and routine fertilization. Grapes can be trained and contained to limit size without a too-disastrous limitation of fruit. Kiwis, with their rampant growth, respond to careful tying and training.

¶Research the required standard spacing in garden books and from experts, and assess your own area to calculate the minimum space required for a home garden. Remember that most plants produce more fruit than an average household can consume. Radical pruning to overcome space limitations can give you the pleasures of homegrown fruit without having to waste it.

FROST PROTECTION

Hardy and *tender* are two words tossed around by gardeners to roughly distinguish how well a plant withstands cold. Tender plants cannot tolerate cold temperatures, because water freezing in the plant tissue expands, damaging or destroying the plant. Hardy plants stand up to a certain amount of cold and are often described as hardy to a certain temperature, for example, "hardy to 32°F." Half-hardy plants will usually survive a cold spell, but may not survive extended cold weather.

¶Some fruits that bud out and bloom early can have fruit production limited by early frosts. If you anticipate this problem, plant the questionable plants in a location where the buds have a chance to revive before the sun hits them. A north- or west-facing exposure may help to save a crop.

¶Woven row covers, a synthetic material that a gardener can use to cover smaller plants, are a good defense weapon against early and late frosts. Rain and light can penetrate but heat is trapped, as in a greenhouse, helping to protect the plants against unseasonable cold.

SELF-STERILE PLANTS

In order for a fruit to form, a flower must be pollinated. Some trees are self-fruitful, meaning they pollinate themselves, but others are self-sterile. In this case, you must buy another cultivar for pollination to occur. A cultivar is a named plant that has been purposely bred to exhibit specific characteristics, from the number of chilling hours to disease resistance. (Cultivar names are enclosed in single quotation marks, such as a 'Surecrop' blueberry.) Cherries are a good example of fruit that needs two different cultivars. If space is limited, plant two trees in the same hole, pruning the trees as if they were one.

PLANTING FOR SUCCESSIVE HARVESTS

When choosing a fruit plant, look to see whether it is an early, mid-, or late-season fruit. Consider all the different fruits in your garden, and plan new selections in terms of spreading the harvest over the whole summer, so no day goes by without some delectable fruit to pick. When a plant needs a pollinator, however, you must pick another cultivar that blooms simultaneously to assure pollination.

CONTAINERS

Adventurous gardeners everywhere are determined to grow plants not at all suited to their climate or their available garden space. Cold-winter gardeners may need a greenhouse to grow figs or oranges, but gardeners with little space can grow almost any type of fruiting plant in a container.

¶The shape of a pot affects the amount of room roots have to grow. Square pots hold a larger volume of potting mix than cylindrical pots with sloping sides. The larger the volume of potting mix, the more room roots have to develop, resulting in a strong, healthy plant that performs well.

¶A large plant needs a large pot. The

larger the plant, the more extensive its root system. Regularly check the drainage hole of your containers to see if roots are beginning to show, indicating that they have begun to fill the container. For the maximum continued growth of the plant, repot when roots show at the bottom. The lack of a drainage hole, a saucer filled with water, or a layer of crockery at the bottom of a pot prevents proper drainage and can cause roots to suffocate. Though it is traditional to add rocks or crockery to the bottom of containers, they may inhibit the drainage of water, so ignore that century-old instruction and just fill the container up with potting mix.

¶Containers planted with sterile potting mix offer a plant no nutrition, for the mix is basically inert. Even containers with some soil or compost in their mix may not hold enough nutrition to feed the plant over its lifetime. Adding fertilizer to the mix replaces missing or used-up nutrients. Studies have shown that potted plants grow better with doses of liquid fertilizer every 2 weeks, but realistically, many busy gardeners find applying liquid fertilizer once a month the best they can do. This monthly program, in conjunction with slow-release granules added to the potting mix when planting, is a good compromise that brings satisfactory results. Always water before you add the liquid fertilizer, as adding liquid fertilizer to dry soil can burn delicate feeder roots.

WATERING PRACTICES

The greatest challenge of container gardening is keeping pots sufficiently watered throughout the year. Because water so critically affects the life of a plant, particularly one in a container, water your plants consistently. A drip system on an automatic timer with a separate mister attached to each container is an easy and effective way to keep container plants well watered. Although you can somewhat disguise the tubing by bringing it up the back of the container, if you insert a tube up through the drainage hole when the pot is planted, it will be almost invisible. The plant must be raised on bricks or blocks so the tubing is not crimped.

¶ If you do not put your plants on a drip, make sure to water them regularly, checking with your finger to see that the potting mix is thoroughly moist throughout after watering. You may need to drench the pot several times for better absorption or take further steps if the root ball has dehydrated. The mix should be moist deep under the surface so the roots can receive water. If the weather becomes windy or hot—which increases the amount of water a plant uses— increase your watering.

POTTING MIXES

Choosing the right mix for the type of plants you raise is essential for healthy root growth and, subsequently, healthy plants. Garden soil alone, scooped into pots out of the ground without careful attention to amendments, may not drain well enough in pots to keep your plants alive. In some locales, garden soil in a container forms a hard soil block, inhibiting water penetration. Untreated garden soil, brought inside, can also produce odors and insects.

REPOTTING FOR THE LONG TERM

To keep potted fruit plants healthy, repot them yearly. Fresh potting mix tossed with slow-release fertilizer gives a plant a fresh start for the following year. When repotting, examine the roots. The overgrown roots of a potbound plant encircling the root ball must be trimmed back and spread out when repotting. Try to untangle and trim back any massed roots. Cut the circling roots back so that when you repot, you can set them straight into the container without bunching or twisting them. The feeder roots, which grow from the tips of the main roots, will regrow quite quickly. Add mix to the bottom and the sides of the container, positioning the top of the root ball 1 inch below the rim of the container. Pat the mix down firmly to make sure there are no air pockets and water thoroughly.

WINTER CARE

Container-bound plants have their roots relatively exposed, for although they are encased in a pot, they are above ground and therefore more susceptible to weather changes. Cold weather can crack an unglazed terra-cotta pot as well as chill the roots and kill the plant. You can cover the pot with burlap and heap it with straw or wood chips, or you can move it to a sheltered site where it will stay cool but not freeze.

¶One of the joys of gardening in pots is the ability to grow plants not suited to the winter temperature of the garden. Figs grown in Minnesota can simply be carried inside to winter over, protected from the subzero temperatures outside. Depending on your climate, the south-

facing wall of a house with an overhanging roof can provide protection and winter warmth for hardy plants. An attached garage or porch will also shelter plants that can take some cold. Dormant deciduous fruit trees in containers do not need sunlight over the winter. After the leaves drop, they can be stored in a dark place such as a windowless room or a basement until spring, although the temperatures of the storage area should not fall below their tolerance. Water them lightly once a month during dormancy.

¶Citrus trees and other evergreens that keep their leaves need sunlight over the winter. However, some citruses require winter chilling, so they will not flourish inside in warm rooms over the winter. Although they should be protected from frosts, they require cool winter temperatures.

PESTS

Because fruit is designed to be attractive to a number of different creatures, you can bet that others will take a personal interest in your harvest. The resultant damage to the fruit or to the plant may be extensive. Wire circles around the trunks of trees are necessary to inhibit rodents and deer from nibbling the bark. Planting trees in wire

baskets can deter gopher damage, although baskets that are too small will inhibit root development.

BIRDS AND SQUIRRELS

Those of us who love feathered and furry friends may suddenly discover depths of rage when a much-anticipated fruit crop begins to disappear, carried away in beaks and paws. Hungry birds can spoil vast numbers of fruit by poking holes in them. Netting large trees may be difficult, but it is necessary. Row cloth, a transparent material that absorbs water and sunlight, works well on shrubs. Encasing clusters of grapes in paper bags or covering low trellises with row covers also works well.

INSECTS

A variety of different pests may attack your plants, although well-watered and -nourished healthy plants appear to have an increased immunity. Try to identify the problem first before you use any sprays or poisons, because insecticides work only for specific types of pests. Take the affected plant or leaves to your local nursery for identification.

¶A number of insects, such as aphids and mites, can be washed away with a brisk spray of water, repeating as necessary.

Aphids are farmed by ants, so encircling the trunk of a tree or shrub with Vaseline or the commercially available Tanglefoot keeps ants away and diminishes the problem. Try the new series of organic soap-based pesticides that suffocate pests with fatty acids harmless to people and animals. Research commercially available biological controls, such as lacewings and trichogramma wasps (very tiny and not like their larger annoying relatives), which attack plant pests without bothering you. Although protecting your harvest by organic methods may be more labor-intensive, the production of safe and nutritious food for yourself and your family is a clear incentive.

SLUGS AND SNAILS

These creatures, particularly bothersome to strawberries and citruses, can become persistent in the spring or fall or during other moist conditions. One of the easiest ways to inhibit them is to use copper tape to encircle the trunk. When a slug or snail attempts to cross it, a chemical reaction produces a shock, stopping them from continuing. Alternatively, maintain a vigilant watch, going out in the evening with a flashlight to hand-pick slugs and snails into a bag containing several generous scoops of salt and discarding it, tightly tied, into the garbage.

¶Commercial fruit growers spray their trees regularly to gain the largest harvest possible. Incidents of disease clusters among orchard workers, however, have caused concern about these practices. In the home garden, it is even more important to minimize the use of poisons. Organic gardeners find that keeping the soil well fertilized and the plant watered to minimize stress lessens the incidence of disease or insect attack. Choosing disease-resistant varieties adds to protection.

¶Organic fruit tending takes a bit more research into alternative control methods, but the health of your family and neighborhood, much less that of the planet, merits the extra attention.

Pruning Basics

Although tomes have been written on the subject, pruning need not be daunting. Some gardeners avoid nursery aisles of fruiting plants because rumor has it that the labors of pruning are too strenuous and technical for the home gardener. Don't be similarly put off; pruning can be as intensive or as relaxed as you wish. Pruning simply shapes the plant so that it forms a framework for healthy fruit. Some gardeners prune for shape only in late winter, tidying up with a trimming in summer. Other types like to study manuals and, armed to the teeth with saws, shears, loppers, and clippers, spend a happy weekend sculpting a masterpiece.

¶If you feel nervous, comfort yourself with the fact that, as with many endeavors, you will only improve with practice. There is also comfort in the fact that underpruning does less damage to most plants than overpruning. Unpruned plants continue to fruit, although they do not have the neat appearance that makes them welcome in small gardens, and in some cases, the fruit and yield may be smaller. Still, skipping a season when life gets too busy to prune won't ruin your plants, and you can easily redress the problem when you have more time.

¶Pruning becomes much simpler if you measure the eventual mature size of a plant against the site where you intend to plant it. Hoping that a standard tree grows slowly in a small space is planning for extra work in the future. Select the appropriate size plant to fit your space.

¶A few general maxims can guide both the novice and the casual expert through the pruning process, and they are applicable to most horticultural situations.

- Prune off dead, dying, diseased, or cracked and broken branches to discourage the spread of disease or insect infestation through rotting wood.
- Take out branches that cross through the center of the tree. Prune branches that rub on each other, causing open wounds in the bark that encourage insect infestation.
- Cut out rooted suckers (sprouts that grow out of the ground from the roots) or vertical-growing water sprouts (fast-growing sprouts that shoot straight upward).
- Prune to an outward-facing bud for a compact framework of branches less likely to break. Also called "heading back branches," this means pruning to a bud that as it matures, will grow directly out of the center of the tree, not across branches or into the center of the tree.

¶To simplify the process, realize that you can, and often should, prune your plants all year long; disabuse yourself of the notion of once-a-year exhausting pruning sessions just before the plants leaf out. Winter pruning, when plants are dormant, allows you to see the plant's overall skeleton so you can make adjustments to the plant's form. However, winter pruning spurs vigorous growth of water sprouts. Mid- to late-summer pruning should be less rigorous, but the plant's response will also be less vigorous, without the excessive growth that occurs in the spring.

¶There are two kinds of pruning cuts. *Thinning cuts* trim branches back to the central trunk to make a compact frame or, in the case of soft fruits, trim the plant down to the ground. *Heading cuts* trim back to a bud or a branch to shorten the main branch and aim the new, emerging growth in the direction you feel benefits the overall shape. Regardless of the type of cut, make sure your tools are razor sharp to avoid tearing the bark or leaving splintered cuts that make the plant vulnerable to insect penetration. Hardware stores often offer inexpensive sharpening services, or you can use a whetstone to keep your tools in top condition.

¶Use a tool appropriate to the diameter of the branch. Hand pruners trim branches up to $3/4$ of an inch. Racheting clippers help gardeners with less hand strength cut

through small branches. Loppers cut up to 2-inch-wide branches, while saws can tackle branches 2 to 3 inches in diameter. Straining to cut a branch larger than a tool's capability can dull the blade or throw the tool out of alignment. Often, such cuts end up savaging the branch, leaving it splintered and rough, and vulnerable for invasion from wood-eating insects.

¶Thinning cuts on trees, particularly when taking out large branches, should be done in three stages, cutting a heavy branch first halfway back to the trunk, then making a second cut halfway between the first cut and the trunk. Make the third cut to avoid the overly heavy limb tearing off before the cut is complete and damaging the bark. The position of the cut is important to avoid excess injury to the plant. Every branch has a curl or ripple of bark just where it joins the main trunk. This curl, called the branch collar, contains chemicals that naturally inhibit rot. If you cut a branch flat against the trunk, you remove the collar and its disease-fighting abilities. Cut off the branch about ¹/₂ inch away from the collar and at an angle with the closest edge at the top of the cut. This allows the rain to run off and prevents it from puddling within the cut to rot the wood.

TERMINAL BUDS AND LATERAL BUDS

All the plant's growth occurs in the terminal buds and lateral buds. The terminal buds, at the tips of the branch, cause the stem to grow in length. The lateral buds grow along the sides of the stem and produce sideways growth, called lateral growth, or just laterals. Terminal buds produce a hormone that inhibits the growth of lateral buds. When you prune a terminal bud, you stop the growth of the stem and encourage the growth of a lateral bud, which may consequently grow out to become a terminal bud. There are also dormant buds, visible bumps on the branches that may be stimulated through pruning to burst out.

¶Water sprouts and suckers are two types of growth that must be pruned out because otherwise they will drain the tree's resources while looking unsightly. Water sprouts grow up vertically from the trunk or branch, sometimes as a response to winter pruning, sometimes as a normal development. These should pruned, but if there are a great many of them growing in response to a winter pruning, wait until late summer to take them all out. Summer pruning retards their growth.

¶Suckers spring up from roots and should

be pruned back. In the case of grafted fruit trees, sometimes the grafted stem dies back and suckers from below the stem grow up in its stead. Growth from the rootstock rarely produces edible fruit, if any at all, having been selected for root vigor, not excellence of fruit.

¶The tarlike substances said to speed the healing of pruning cuts, while salves to the gardener's conscience, in actuality retard healing. In fact, they may leave the plant more vulnerable to rot and insects and should not be used. A good cut at the right time of year is the best prevention.

FRUITING GROWTH PATTERNS

Deciduous fruit trees bear fruit in two different ways. Understanding the growth patterns allows you to prune accordingly so you don't cut off the wood that produces fruit.

SPUR TYPES

Pomes and stone fruits produce stubby growth off of branches that produce the blooms that lead to fruit. These are different from leafing branches, which do not produce fruit. After some practice, you will be able to identify these fruiting spurs while the tree is dormant, for they look different from the short branches that only produce leaves. Each type of tree has a slightly different-appearing spur, so learn to spot those on each type of tree. The spurs can live and produce fruit for a number of years, depending on the type of tree.

TERMINAL BUD TYPES

Citrus, quince, walnut, chestnut, persimmon, mulberry, fig, and pomegranate trees and cane fruits are terminal bearing, which means they flower only on new growth, at the end of the shoot.

PRUNING YOUNG FRUIT TREES

The pruning of young trees just being set into the garden differs from the annual pruning of an established tree. Over-enthusiastic pruning of young trees actually retards fruiting for up to several seasons, although some pruning is necessary to select the scaffolding of permanent branches.

¶When at the nursery, choose a tree with limbs nicely spaced around the trunk. Be sure to check the distance between the limbs you are selecting for the main scaffolding. The limbs should be equally distributed around the tree moving up the trunk. For home use, a low-branching tree, which is easier to harvest, is preferable to one with higher branches unless the siting of the tree, such as along a walkway, makes higher branches necessary.

¶Prune off branches as necessary to space them at least 4 inches apart. Select branches growing out from the main stem at a 45- to 65-degree angle, because they will grow stronger than those with a tighter angle. When the limb is loaded with fruit, a wider-angle branch bears the weight with minimal cracking or breaking. Toothpicks or even clothespins spread between the trunk and the branches will train them to grow to a wider angle. Insert these spreaders in the spring, when the branches are still soft and supple.

¶Customarily, fruit trees are pruned to three different shapes, regardless of how tall the final tree will be. Open-center pruning, modified open-center pruning, and central-leader pruning are the standard forms.

OPEN-CENTER PRUNING

In the open-center style, the upright leader, or upper part of the trunk, is cut to encourage the growth of outer branches while leaving the center of the tree open. In this style, also known as the "vase," the

short trunk of the open center lets in plenty of light for excellent fruit ripening as well as good air circulation to inhibit rusts and fungal diseases. Open-center pruning limits the growth of the tree and thus is helpful in diminishing the height of standard-sized trees. Generally, stone fruits are pruned to this style.

¶When pruning to the open center, make sure that the scaffolding has excellent wide-angled branches because weaker branches, when laden with fruit, can split open, breaking the tree in half. Although some orchardists prop their trees as a precaution, this makes extra work and isn't always successful.

¶To shape a tree in the open-center style, cut back the upright leader to about 24 inches above the ground. However, if the leader has a developed system of branches, look first to see that there are enough branches underneath your cut to send out a strong scaffolding. Position your cut above enough branches or buds to allow good branch development. Cut back the branches to about 5 inches from the trunk. In the following years, keep pruning back half the year's growth—seen by the color change on the bark—to lateral buds to encourage branching of the scaffolding.

MODIFIED OPEN-CENTER PRUNING

Because the open-center pruning style can cause a mature tree to split open, the modified, or delayed, open-center style was devised to accomplish the same central openness but with less of a tendency to split. Cut off the central leader at 24 inches the first year, then train one branch upward from those that sprout out at the cut, as if to replace the cut trunk. The branch may need to be directed straight up, in which case attach a stick with string alongside the new leader and then again farther down the trunk to rigidly direct the leader upward. The second spring, prune back this leader to half the previous year's growth and train another to take its place as before. The third year, prune this leader, making sure no further branches take its place. This "delayed" open center makes a stronger tree, with scaffolding around the two previous cuts.

¶Always prune back any side shoots underneath the central leader so they never become taller than the leader.

CENTRAL-LEADER PRUNING

Central-leader pruning gives you a strong, upward-growing tree—similar in shape to a Christmas tree—which is useful with smaller trees that need less pruning to keep them to a manageable size. The strong trunk easily holds the heavy weight of the fruit and, by spacing branches, enough light penetrates through the canopy for excellent fruit ripening.

¶Use a dwarf or semi-dwarf tree for this style, or the tree will soon grow beyond ladder reach. The vertical branches are pruned back to a series of tiers, grouping the branches along the trunk with enough space in between each group, at least 18 to 36 inches, to let light into the center of the tree. Every year the central leader is pruned back one half of its growth from the previous season. A change in color and texture along the upper trunk indicates a new season's growth. Make sure that the resulting shoot grows straight up. If it doesn't, tie on a stick to keep it pointing straight upward.

PRUNING MATURE FRUIT TREES

Fruit trees in back gardens must be pruned to fit the space, sometimes sacrificing an amount of fruit. Because the supply of fruit usually exceeds what one family can consume, however, such pruning leaves plenty of harvest. Summer pruning may be more useful on mature

trees than winter pruning, for it does not encourage the wealth of growth that results after winter pruning.

¶If a tree has been neglected, several years may be needed to gradually bring it back to trim. Be cautious: Overpruning the first year can let so much light into the interior that the tree will develop sunscald. The first winter, prune off some of the too-large branches to bring light into the canopy, and use heading cuts to shorten the limbs. Cut out any dead or crossing wood. In late summer, prune out the excess growth from the winter pruning and continue to shape the tree, gradually pruning back the branches and lowering the canopy. Continue the pruning regime the next several years, gradually restoring the tree to a graceful and purposeful shape.

PRUNING SHAPED TREES: ESPALIER

Fruit trees have long been shaped to produce as much fruit as possible in a limited area, for home gardeners have always been chary of wasting garden room. Since early times, fruit trees have had to be squeezed inside castle walls or within walled towns to protect them from wild and domesticated animals, much less passing armies. Fruit domesticated within

private gardens, from the roof gardens along the Euphrates at the time of the hanging gardens of Babylon to the early Greek and Roman family enclaves, always needed to fit the available space. Woven fences, hedgerows, fans, arches, and cordons of fruit trees combined form and function. Follow the example of these clever gardeners while adding living architectural effects to your garden with the bonus of flowers and fruits.

¶There are any number of complicated and exotic shapes, but it is best to begin simply with the placement of a fruit tree against a wall. Your basic goal is to prune and thin branches into a two-dimensional form. A T shape, with branches spread at right angles along wires, is one of the easiest forms. Run 3 wires spaced at 18-inch intervals along a fence or wall. Cut off the central leader of a bare-root tree just below the first wire. As the branches sprout out at the point of the cut through the early spring, choose 3. The center branch should be trained vertically by fastening it at the wires as it grows upward, while the ones on either side are tied down to the wire horizontally with clear grafting ribbon or inconspicuous green sisal. Do not make ties so tight they bite into the soft bark, and make sure to leave

room for the branch to grow in girth. To train a tree against a masonry or brick wall, search out masonry nails with special bendable tips. The second winter pruning, cut the central leader just below the second wire, and cut the lateral branches on the first wire back to 18 inches. Repeat the procedure the third year, and thereafter cut off any shoots from the center branch. Continue to prune the horizontal laterals just to balance the form. Be forewarned that peaches and nectarines, which fruit on new wood, are exceedingly difficult to espalier to maintain an elegant form and produce a good quantity of fruit.

VINES

Annual vines need no pruning, just some direction to keep the vines from growing so closely that they limit air circulation, encouraging the mildew diseases to which they are susceptible.

¶Perennial vines must be pruned to encourage new fruit wood, which grows on old wood in some plants and on new wood in others. Make sure to determine the growth pattern of the vine before you prune.

BRAMBLES

Brambles generally fruit on old wood, and with some, the canes die after they fruit. Others, however, continue to fruit, although with less harvest, so old canes are pruned to increase the amount of fruit. Thin canes to 3 to 6 inches apart for good air circulation to avoid fungal diseases.

SHRUBS

Blueberries, gooseberries, and currants need little pruning, for most fruit on old wood. Branches need to be thinned and old wood taken out to increase fruitfulness, however. Check the growth pattern of the shrub and prune for fruiting vigor.

CITRUS TREES

Citrus trees need little pruning beyond the basics of balancing the tree and opening the canopy to encourage ripening. Citruses bear fruit at the terminals, so if you prune heavily you may cut out the fruiting buds.

These basic instructions will get you started pruning. As you gain confidence you may wish to study books that focus exclusively on pruning. Some of the refinements of girdling, pleaching, and intricate espalier can provide gardeners much pleasure after they have mastered the basics.

POTTED
FRUIT

Fruiting plants are usually among those on the "if I only had more room" list, but quite unfairly so. A number of fruiting plants grow satisfactorily in pots, producing foliage, flowers, and fruit. Strawberries are admirably suited to window boxes and can be grown along railings; small fruit trees bear productively in containers, and grapes can clamber up a wall out of a half barrel. ❧ Of course, gardening in containers is challenging, for plants so confined need extra care. A good drip system or a rigid watering schedule is essential to keep them healthy and productive in their limited world, for water essential for bloom and fruit growth and to avoid excessive fruit drop. Consider supplementing your potting soil with polymers, small grains that swell up when soaked with water and allow the roots to absorb it as needed. Regular applications of liquid fertilizer are necessary to replace the nutrients that leach out from the frequent watering. Fruiting plants need at least 4 to 6 hours of direct sun a day. If sunlight is a problem, consider putting your plants on wheeled platforms so you can move them into sunnier spots as the light changes throughout the year. A south-facing wall gets the most sun in winter, though it may be shaded in the summer. ❧ As plants grow larger, they require bigger pots, so repotting yearly is important to keep a plant maturing. At some point, the gardener decides the pot size cannot grow larger. The plants will continue to thrive, but a yearly pruning of the roots will be necessary, for a pot-bound plant, with its roots encircling the root ball, will not continue to produce fruit. If the pot is large, top dress the plant: Dig out as much mix as possible and add new mix and an application of slow-release organic fertilizer granules to set the plant up for another year of success. In a few years, however, the plant will have to be root pruned to continue productivity.

HARVEST OF STRAWBERRIES

Strawberries seldom succeed in those abysmal terra-cotta containers called strawberry pots, for the plants dry out far too quickly. The plants grow well, however, in containers with more root room, a generous amount of high-nitrogen fertilizer, and plenty of water. Watch out for pests. ¶ The taste of a strawberry is determined by both variety and growing conditions, particularly temperature. Don't overwater the plants when the fruit is coloring up, for excess water dilutes the flavor of the berries. ¶ Strawberries are hardy perennials but grow in two distinct patterns. The June-bearing types ripen almost simultaneously, while the everbearers fruit, albeit less copiously, later in the summer and continue to do so until fall. Look carefully at a plant to find the area where the leaves sprout at the top of the roots, called the crown. Set in the plants so that the crown is just above soil level, for if below, it rots, and if above, the roots dry out quickly; either way the plant dies. Plant bare-root strawberries early in spring, or set out potted starters. ¶ Strawberries spread by runners, which can be pinched off the mother plant and rooted in new pots. Simply snuggle the new plant down into the mix and keep it well watered. After 3 years, discard the original plants, for the harvest will diminish. ¶ **HOW TO DO IT** ¶ Whether using bare-root plants or starts (plants in potting mix), first submerge them in a deep sink or bucket of water until the roots are soaked or the air stops bubbling out of the container. Moisten the potting mix thoroughly. ¶ Measure the quantity of mix needed to fill each pot and add the correct amount of slow-release fertilizer granules according to the manufacturer's instructions. Add enough mix to the bottom of each container to bring the top of the root ball to 5 inches below the rim of the pot. Space 4 plants equally around the rim of each container. Scoop out

Strawberry
Fragaria *species*

What You Need
1 dozen bare-root plants or starts
3 containers, each 18 inches wide
by 20 inches deep
Potting mix
All-purpose slow-release organic
fertilizer granules
Organic compost
All-purpose liquid organic fertilizer

Pollination Requirements
Self-fertile

Light Conditions
4 to 6 hours or more of full sun

Growth Pattern
Plants fruit for 3 years; runners can be potted up to replace mother plants

Pruning
Pinch off runners early in growing season; let later runners develop fruit

Fruit Thinning
Not necessary

Hardiness
Hardy to 0°F

Chill Requirement
200 to 300 hours

enough mix to make a planting hole. ¶ For bare-root plants, make a little pyramid of mix in the middle of the hole, spreading the roots over the top. Set starts with each root ball in the planting hole. For both types, add mix around the sides, tamping down as you go, continuing to add mix until it reaches the top of the roots but is below the level of the crown. Water again thoroughly, and add more mix if the level drops. Mulch the top of the mix with 3 inches of organic compost. ¶ Place the containers in a shady place for the plants to recover, watering daily for 5 days, before placing them in their permanent site. Water consistently to keep the potting mix moist but not soggy, and fertilize once a month with a liquid organic fertilizer diluted to half strength according to the manufacturer's instructions.

Citrus tree

Ever since Juno wore a crown of orange blossoms to seduce Jupiter, the fragrance of citrus has symbolized romance and love. ¶ Columbus brought oranges, lemons, and limes to the New World, where they thrived in the warm, tropical climate. Spanish missionaries cultivated orchards of sweet oranges and lemons in both California and Florida. ¶ Today, citrus fruits are grafted to dwarf rootstocks, so although full-sized trees can reach 20 feet, smaller trees grow well in containers. Meyer lemons are the most hardy citrus, but there are many other unusual types, such as the kumquat, calamondin, and blood orange. Citruses are purchased in nursery containers, from 1-gallon cans up to larger specimens. ¶ In warm-winter areas, citrus can be grown outside all year long. To protect tender citruses from winter frosts, bring them inside to a bright, sunny room where the temperature doesn't drop below 50°F. Check the specific growing requirements of your citrus, for some require cool winter temperatures and won't thrive in a warm living room. ¶ **HOW TO DO IT** ¶ Transplant the citrus from its nursery container into a pot that is at least 4 inches larger all around than the root ball of the plant. Submerge the plant in its container in a deep sink or bucket of water until the air stops bubbling out of the container. ¶ Moisten the potting mix thoroughly. Measure the quantity of mix needed to fill the new pot, taking into account the size of the plant's root ball, and add the correct amount of slow-release fertilizer granules according to the manufacturer's instructions. Add enough mix to the bottom of the container to bring the top of the root ball to 1 inch below the rim of the pot. Slide the citrus out of its container and position the root ball in the middle of the new pot. Add mix around the sides, tamping down as you go, continuing to add mix until it reaches the top of the root ball. Water thoroughly and add more mix if the sides slump below the

Citrus
Dwarf Improved Meyer Lemon: C. meyeri;
Dwarf Grapefruit: Citrus x paradisi;
Dwarf Mandarin Orange:
reticulata Blanco

What You Need
Citrus in gallon pot • Container 4 inches larger in circumference than plant's root ball • Potting mix • All-purpose slow-release organic fertilizer granules • All-purpose liquid organic fertilizer

Pollination Requirements
Self-pollinating

Light Conditions
4 to 6 hours or more of full sun

Growth Pattern
Terminal

Pruning
Prune to shape and balance plant, root prune potted plants yearly when desired size has been achieved

Fruit Thinning
Not necessary

Hardiness
Some hardy to 10°F

Chill Requirement
None, but most require cool winter temperatures

level of the root ball. ¶ Move the plant out of bright light to recover, watering it daily for 5 days. Place the plant in the warmest, sunniest spot in the garden. Water consistently to keep the potting mix moist but not soggy, and fertilize once a month until September with liquid organic fertilizer diluted to half strength according to the manufacturer's instructions.

POTTED FIG

Figs have been relished for thousands of years. An Egyptian tomb painting from 1900 B.C. shows trained monkeys picking figs for their masters. Though commonly thought to grow in only warm-winter gardens, some varieties can survive down to about 10°F, and even frost-damaged plants usually sprout back, fruiting that summer on new wood. If you live in a snowy climate, consider a fig grown in a container, which you can bring inside to winter over in a cool room or even a dark basement—dormant plants don't need light. ¶ The fig is well qualified to live in a container, for it tolerates abysmal conditions of poor soil, hot temperatures, and lack of water. If you want your fig to bear copiously, though, care should be taken to keep it well watered and nourished. Look for a fig on dwarf rootstock, and root prune yearly when the plant has reached its mature size. ¶ An uncommon fruit, the flowers of the fig are borne inside it. Normally, a fig tree bears two harvests, one in the summer from fruits set the previous fall, and one in the fall. Although the commonly available Black Mission, with its burgundy-colored flesh, and the pink-fleshed Adriatic fruits are delicious, look for some of the less well-known varieties that can succeed in your climate. Their flavors can range from honey-sweet to a citrusy tang. ¶ **HOW TO DO IT** ¶ Transplant the fig from its nursery container into a pot that is at least 4 inches larger all around than the root ball of the plant. Submerge the plant in its container in a deep sink or bucket of water until the air stops bubbling out of the container. Check the root ball, pruning back any broken or overly long roots. Moisten the potting mix thoroughly. ¶ Measure the quantity of mix needed to fill the new pot, taking into account the size of the plant's root ball, and add the correct amount of slow-release organic fertilizer granules according to the manufacturer's ✐

Fig
Ficus
❧

What You Need
Fig in gallon pot
Container 4 inches larger in circumference
than plant's root ball
Potting mix
All-purpose slow-release organic
fertilizer granules
All-purpose liquid organic fertilizer
❧

Pollination Requirements
Self-pollinating
❧

Light Conditions
4 to 6 hours or more of full sun
❧

Growth Pattern
Terminal
❧

Pruning
Prune to central leader, cut back root suckers, and root prune potted plants yearly
when desired size has been achieved
❧

Fruit Thinning
Not necessary
❧

Hardiness
Some hardy to 10°F
❧

Chill Requirement
100 to 500 hours, depending on variety
❧

instructions. Add enough mix to the bottom of the container to bring the top of the root ball to 1 inch below the rim of the pot. Slide the fig out of its container and position the root ball in the middle of the new pot. Add mix around the sides, tamping down as you go, continuing to add mix until it reaches the top of the root ball. Water thoroughly and add more mix if the sides slump below the level of the root ball. ¶ Move the plant out of bright light to recover, watering it daily for 5 days. Place the plant in the warmest, sunniest spot in the garden. Water consistently to keep the potting mix moist but not soggy, and fertilize once a month until September with liquid organic fertilizer according to the manufacturer's instructions.

Icebox Watermelons

Watermelons originated in Africa, where the fruit of the wild species grows only to the size of an orange. To save garden space, watermelons can be easily grown in a large container set into a location with 6 hours of sun. Provide copious quantities of water during the early growing period, a rich potting mix combined with an abundant amount of organic compost, and additional feedings of liquid fertilizer. A thick mulch helps maintain the warm temperature of the mix as well as conserving moisture. New varieties include yellow-fleshed and seedless melons, which must be grown with a seeded melon type as a pollinator to ensure fruiting. ¶ Harvest when the skin color where the melon rests on the ground changes from green to yellow and the tendrils on either side of the melon have shriveled. ¶ **HOW TO DO IT** ¶ Plant your watermelon seeds outside after the last chance of frost has passed, or start them inside 4 weeks before you plan to set out warm-weather crops such as tomatoes. Soak the seeds in water for up to 12 hours before planting. ¶ Measure the quantity of potting mix to almost fill the pot and add the correct amount of slow-release fertilizer granules according to the manufacturer's instructions. Moisten the mix thoroughly, tossing it to evenly distribute the granules. Add mix to the pot to fill it to 1 inch below the rim. Plant 6 seeds in each pot, evenly spaced around the rim. With your finger or a pencil, make a hole 1 inch deep. Drop in the seed, cover it with mix, and tamp it down. Water gently to avoid displacing the seeds. ¶ Place the pot outdoors where it will receive 6 hours of sun daily. When the seeds have sprouted and grown 5 inches high, thin to the strongest 3 plants. Mulch up to the rim with organic compost. Water consistently to keep the mix moist but not soggy, and fertilize every 2 weeks with a liquid organic fertilizer diluted to half strength according to the manufacturer's instructions.

Icebox Watermelons
Citrullus lanatus: 'Sugar Baby', 'Tiger Baby', 'Yellow Doll', 'Yellow Cutie'

What You Need
Watermelon seeds • Potting mix • All-purpose slow-release organic fertilizer granules • Container, 24 inches wide by 20 inches deep, or a half barrel 28 inches wide by 18 inches deep • Organic compost • All-purpose liquid organic fertilizer

Pollination Requirements
Self-pollinating

Light Conditions
6 hours or more of full sun

Growth Pattern
Long vining arms, fruit in 65 to 75 days depending on variety

Pruning
Unnecessary

Fruit Thinning
Pinch out growing tips and take off undersized melons 1 month before end of growing season to encourage larger melons to ripen before first frost

Hardiness
Tender

Chill Requirement
None

VINES AND

BRAMBLES

The long, pliable branches of vining fruit plants fairly drip with bounty. The nature of their growth makes them responsive to being trained on fences, up arbors, along walls, or over gar-

den sheds. Like the wayward child, these plants need supervision to keep them from tangling, twining, and twisting into knots. ❧ Annual vines are much easier to keep an eye on. Although they grow with wild abandon, given sufficient space they don't trip over themselves too badly. At the beginning of summer, the gardener can separate and direct the stems, using a pliable stick bent to a V-shape to set each one on track and keep it from ensnaring its neighbor. Separating the stems helps maintain good air circulation and thus prevents fungal diseases. ❧ Perennial vines also grow with great vigor, and must be pruned annually to keep them fruiting. Most of them produce astonishingly long stems, some as long as 30 feet, so finding the right space for them and providing a strong trellis or fence that can support the weight of the branches is essential. ❧ Brambles are biennials, meaning they produce fruit on old wood during the second season. Tracking canes that have borne fruit so they can be pruned at the end of the season can be quite tricky, so take the advice of garden expert Robert Kourik and plant beds of berries to prune in alternate years. If you have four beds of berries, after fruiting, prune two beds down to the ground one year, and the next year prune the other two beds, letting the first two develop to fruit the following year. This system greatly simplifies the process of pruning selectively. ❧ The recommended spacing distances for these plants can be lessened if the gardener is willing to spend a bit of extra time each fall digging out beds that have become too crowded, then pruning back stems each spring. The recommended space allows the plants to gradually fill in, making less work for the gardener, but don't hesitate to plant a little closer if your garden space demands it.

TABLE GRAPES

Grapes are one of the oldest cultivated fruits in agriculture. Use vertical supports to raise grapes off the ground, thus saving room in the garden beds. An overhead arbor is one of the most pleasant uses of grapevines. Grapes need summer heat, so place them where they will receive at least 6 hours of sun every day. ¶ Although seedless grapes are popular today, don't disregard older seeded varieties like the Muscat with its unforgettable honey-rich flavor. Look also for uncommon varieties; search out Zante grapes, the tiny grapes used for champagne, which dry to currant size, and manookas, which make extraordinarily large raisins. Grapes are sensitive to climate and soil conditions, so check with your local nursery or extension service for the varieties that do best in your area. ¶ Don't forget that the new leaves, still tender in late spring, can be pickled in a salt brine to make edible wraps. ¶ **HOW TO DO IT** ¶ In early spring, purchase your grapevines. Keep the roots damp if you cannot plant the vines immediately. Before planting, remove the wrappings and submerge the roots in a deep sink or bucket of water for 4 to 6 hours. Check the root ball, pruning back any broken or overly long roots. ¶ Dig a hole in a sunny location just big enough to fit in the root mass with the top of the root ball at soil level and 4 inches in front of the trellis, arbor, fence, or wall it will grow on. Make a pyramid of soil in the middle of the hole, spreading the roots over the pyramid. Add soil around the sides, tamping down as you go, continuing to add soil until it reaches the top of the roots. Water again thoroughly, and add more soil if the level drops. Space plants 5 feet apart. Mulch the top of the soil with 3 inches of organic compost. ¶ Water the new plants near the root crown every day for 5 days, then ✒

Grape
Vitus: 'Concord', 'Manooka', 'Zante', 'Perlette', 'Suffolk Red Seedless'

What You Need
6 bare-root grape plants
30 feet of trellis, arbor, fence, or wall
Organic compost
All-purpose slow-release organic fertilizer granules

Pollination Requirements
Self-fertile

Light Conditions
6 hours or more of full sun

Growth Pattern
Long vining branches to 30 feet

Pruning
Do not prune first year, thereafter prune to encourage side branches on 1-year-old wood; in summer, prune back tips to contain size and prune out leaves to open up vine and expose fruit to sunlight

Thinning
Thin fruit to every 6 inches

Hardiness
To 0°F or lower, depending on variety

Chill Requirement
100 to 500 hours, depending on variety

water 12 inches out from the crowns weekly or as needed to keep the soil moist but not soggy. The first year, feed the plants once a month with organic liquid fertilizer diluted according to the manufacturer's instructions. Once the vines are established, they tolerate low-water conditions. ¶ As the plants grow, guide them up into the trellis or arbor or along the fence or wall, making sure their tendrils fasten. Winter prune to cut back side branches and space them about 6 inches along the main trunk. Pinch off tips and leaves throughout the summer as needed to contain the plant's size and keep the vine open to sun and air. In the late winter, scatter slow-release organic fertilizer granules over the bed according to the manufacturer's instructions. Renew the mulch every fall.

Arbor of Kiwi Fruit

The kiwi is a vigorous grower, requiring a strong support for its gangly limbs that can grow to 30 feet long in maturity. Summer pruning keeps the vines untangled, while winter pruning cuts out old wood and trims new wood for continued fruiting. The better-known variety, which produces the fuzzy, egg-shaped kiwi, is tender when young. The hardy variety produces smaller fruit, but certain cultivars can handle temperatures to -40°F. One male plant is necessary to pollinate 8 or fewer female plants. Kiwi fruits will ripen in part shade. ¶ **HOW TO DO IT** ¶ In early spring, purchase your kiwi vines. Keep the roots damp if you cannot plant the vines immediately. Before planting, remove the wrappings and submerge the roots in a deep sink or bucket of water for 4 to 6 hours. Check the root ball, pruning back any broken or overly long roots. ¶ Dig a hole in a sunny location just big enough to fit in the root mass with the top of the root ball at soil level and 4 inches in front of the trellis, arbor, fence, or wall you will train them on. Make a pyramid of soil in the middle of the hole, spreading the roots over it. Add soil around the sides, tamping down as you go, continuing to add soil until it reaches the top of the roots. Water again thoroughly, and add more soil if the level drops. Space plants 5 feet apart. Mulch the top of the soil near the trunk with 3 inches of organic compost. Water the new plants near the trunk every day for 5 days, then water consistently 12 inches out from the trunks to keep the soil moist but not soggy. ¶ As the plants grow, guide them up into the trellis or arbor or attach them along the fence or wall, as they have no fastening tendrils. Winter prune to cut out 4-year-old wood, shorten new branches, and open the vine up to sunlight. In late winter, scatter slow-release organic fertilizer granules over the bed according to the manufacturer's instructions. Renew the mulch every spring.

Hardy Kiwi
Actinidia arguta

Fuzzy Kiwi
Actinidia deliciosa

What You Need
*1 male kiwi plant, 2 female kiwi plants •
30 feet of trellis, arbor, fence, or wall •
Organic compost • All-purpose slow-
release organic fertilizer granules*

Pollination Requirements
Male and female plants

Light Conditions
*4 to 6 hours or more of full sun; can take
some shade in hot summer areas*

Growth Pattern
Long vining branches to 30 feet

Pruning
*Winter prune 4-year-old wood, shorten new
wood, and cut back new growth by one half;
summer prune to untangle crossing branches,
to shape, and to shorten long shoots*

Fruit Thinning
Unnecessary

Hardiness
*Fuzzy kiwi hardy to 0°F when established
and well mulched, hardy kiwi
hardy to -40°F*

Chill Requirement
800 to 900 hours

Orange-fleshed French Cantaloupes

The French cantaloupe called Charantais and its hybrids have gained particular fame for their intense perfume-fragrant flavors. ¶ Most melons require at least 6 hours of direct sun each day, lots of water, and heavy feeding. You can also raise temperatures by planting melons in a raised mound or hill, and by using black plastic to cover the soil. Some melons grow as bush types suitable for container cultivation, while others grow as vines that can be trained up trellises with the fruit supported by fabric slings. ¶ Pick melons when the netting changes color from green to tan and the blossom end exudes a ripe fragrance. Keep melons unrefrigerated and serve at room temperature to enjoy the richest flavor. ¶ **HOW TO DO IT** ¶ Plant your melon seeds outside after the last chance of frost has passed, or start them inside 4 weeks before you plan to set in warm-weather crops such as tomatoes. Soak the seeds in water up to 12 hours before planting. ¶ Dig shovelfuls of organic compost and dried manure into the planting area, mounding up the soil to a hill about 6 inches high and 8 to 10 inches across. Plant 6 seeds in each hill, evenly spaced around the rim. With your finger or a pencil, make a hole 1 inch deep. Drop in the seed, cover it with soil, tamp the soil down, and water. ¶ When the seeds have sprouted and the plants are 4 inches high, thin to the 3 strongest plants. Mulch the hill with organic compost and cover the soil with black plastic to increase the heat. Water consistently to keep the soil moist but not soggy, and fertilize every 2 weeks with a liquid organic fertilizer diluted to half strength according to the manufacturer's instructions.

Orange-Fleshed French Cantaloupe
Cucumis melo, Reticulatus *group:*
'Charantais', 'Savor', 'Acor', Charmel'

What You Need
Melon seeds
Organic compost
Dried composted steer manure
Liquid organic fertilizer

Pollination Requirements
Self-fertile

Light Conditions
6 hours or more of full sun

Growth Pattern
Long vining arms; fruit in 75 to 85 days
depending on variety

Pruning
Unnecessary

Fruit Thinning
Pinch off growing tips and take off under-
sized melons 1 month before end of growing
season to encourage larger melons to ripen
before first frost

Hardiness
Tender

Chill Requirement
none

RED AND YELLOW RASPBERRIES

Raspberries in home gardens are whisked directly to the kitchen, if they are not eaten while they are being picked. Now available is a golden raspberry, with a sweeter taste due to the lack of a balancing acid. The sight of a glass bowl brimming with a mixture of red and gold berries may cause some diners to swoon in anticipation. ¶ Raspberries are renowned in England and Scotland, an indication that they prefer cooler weather. Types have been developed for a variety of climates, however, and in the hotter areas, a partly shady site suits their constitution. The root of the raspberry is perennial, but the canes die back the second year after bearing. Raspberries come in two types, summer-bearing and everbearing. Summer-bearing raspberries are biennials, fruiting generously the summer of the second year. Everbearings boast of bearing raspberries all the time, though in actuality they bear in the fall of the first year and then the next summer. ¶ Because of their different growth patterns, pruning is also slightly different for the two types. Let the summer types produce canes and, in the second season after they have fruited, cut them down to the ground. New growth sprouts up near the cut-off crown. Choose up to a dozen of these sprouts and let them grow. Dig up any additional sprouts, for too many weaken the plant. In the spring, cut the new canes back to 5 feet. The lateral shoots that grow up will bear fruit. ¶ Everbearing raspberries fruit the first year at the top of the cane. Pruning these canes down by one third after fruiting allows them to fruit along the bottom two thirds the next spring. After they have finished fruiting, cut them down to the ground. ¶ Make sure to fertilize the plants during the blooming season and provide plenty of water as the fruits develop. Pruning to keep canes 6 inches apart maintains air circulation and prevents disease. ¶ **HOW TO DO IT** ¶ In late winter, purchase your bare-root berry bushes. Keep the roots damp if you cannot plant the bushes immediately. Before planting, remove the wrappings and submerge the roots in a deep sink or bucket of water for 4 to 6 hours. Check the root ball, pruning back any broken or

Raspberry
Rubus idaeas

What You Need
6 bare-root raspberry plants
15 feet of planting bed
Organic compost
All-purpose slow-release fertilizer granules

Pollination Requirements
Self-fertile

Light Conditions
4 to 6 hours or more of full sun

Growth Pattern
Everbearing: fruit on new canes in fall and following summer; summer-bearing: fruit on biennial canes

Pruning
Prune out fruiting canes at end of season
🦗
Fruit Thinning
Unnecessary
🦗
Hardiness
Hardy
🦗
Chill Requirement
200 hours
🦗

overly long roots. ¶ Dig a hole in a sunny location just big enough to fit in the root mass with the top of the root ball at soil level. Make a pyramid of soil in the middle of the hole, spreading the roots over it. Add soil around the sides, tamping down as you go, continuing to add soil until it reaches the top of the roots. Water again thoroughly, and add more soil if the level drops. Space plants $2\frac{1}{2}$ feet apart in beds with 5 feet between each row. Mulch the top of the soil with 3 inches of organic compost. ¶ Water the new plants near the root crown every day for 5 days, then water consistently 12 inches out from the crowns to keep the soil moist but not soggy. The following fall, scatter slow-release fertilizer granules over the bed according to the manufacturer's instructions. Renew the mulch every fall.

BLACKBERRIES ALONG A FENCE

There are two main types of berries: the thornless, which stands erect; and the thorny, with trailing canes that succeed best when trellised. While the erect varieties are hardy, the trailing types tend to be more tender and can freeze in cold winter climates. In a marginally cold area, cut the canes in late fall and bury the roots in soil with a heavy straw mulch to help them survive the winter. ¶ In early spring, add lots of high-nitrogen fertilizer and mulch heavily, for blackberries are hungry feeders and like moist soil. Drip irrigation is preferable, but if you need to water overhead, make sure to water early in the day so the foliage dries off. ¶ **HOW TO DO IT** ¶ In early spring, purchase your bare-root berry bushes. Keep the roots damp if you cannot plant the bushes immediately. Before planting, remove the wrappings and submerge the roots in a deep sink or bucket of water for 4 to 6 hours. Check the root ball, pruning back any broken or overly long roots. ¶ Dig a hole in a sunny location just big enough to fit in the root mass with the top of the root ball at soil level. Make a pyramid of soil in the middle of the hole, spreading the roots over it. Add soil around the sides, tamping down as you go, continuing to add soil until it reaches the top of the roots. Water again thoroughly, and add more soil if the level drops. Space plants 5 feet apart in beds with 3 feet between each row. Mulch the top of the soil near the crown with 6 inches of organic compost. ¶ Water the new plants near the root crown every day for 5 days, then water consistently 12 inches out from the crowns to keep the soil moist but not soggy. The following fall, scatter slow-release organic fertilizer granules over the bed according to the manufacturer's instructions. Renew the mulch every fall.

Blackberry
Rubus fructicosus: 'Boysenberry', 'Loganberry', 'Ollalie'

❧

What You Need
*6 blackberry plants
30 feet of planting bed
Organic compost
All-purpose slow-release organic fertilizer granules*

❧

Pollination Requirements
Self-fertile

❧

Light Conditions
4 to 6 hours or more of full sun

❧

Growth Pattern
Canes with fruit borne on side shoots the second year

❧

Pruning
Prune out canes that fruited at end of season; trim fruiting side shoots back to 2 inches from stem the fall before they fruit

❧

Fruit Thinning
Unnecessary

❧

Hardiness
Erect types hardy, trailing types tender

❧

Chill Requirement
None

❧

FRUITING

SHRUBS

Fruiting shrubs are ideally suited to fulfill a number of roles in the garden. Their mature size is appropriate to smaller garden spaces— staying at about 5 to 6 feet tall—so they can be grown to define property edges, to draw lines, or to form borders. Their blossoms announce the arrival of spring, and their fruit is set low and is easy to pick. Many shrub fruits are extremely high in vitamins and minerals. Additionally, shrubs are among the easiest of fruiting plants to prune. ❧ A few years ago, the concept of edible landscaping made an appearance on the gardening scene. These plants fall into that category perfectly, combining beauty and utility in the garden with the culinary pleasure yielded by their fruit. Yet most fruiting shrubs haven't earned a place in our fruit gardens, as American gardeners are relatively unfamiliar with using their fruit. More prevalent in European gardens, gooseberries, currants, and pomegranates are less well known than the American perennial favorite, blueberries. These fruits should be tried because they add to the wealth of the fruit garden, and they are not always available in produce markets. ❧ Smaller fruits do take time to pick, but they are so thickly clustered on the branches that a bucket fills quickly. Remembering that the goal of fruit is seed dissemination, you must be prepared to protect your harvest from birds. Netting or row covers may be essential to save the harvest. ❧ Pomegranates and blueberries can be eaten fresh, but currants and some types of very tart gooseberries require cooking. Jams, syrups, ice creams and sorbets, grunts or slumps, fools, and pies are classic ways to use fruits. Adding new ingredients to your repertoire can set off a hunt through cookbooks, with the reward of new dishes. And these shrubs are but a sampling. Check through specialty catalogues for additional fruiting shrubs, such as elderberries, chokeberries, serviceberries, and lingonberries.

BLUEBERRY HEDGE

The thought of blueberries immediately brings to mind blueberry muffins. But who could run out of ideas for ways to eat blueberries, what with jams, syrups, pancakes, scones, pies, fools, ice creams, sorbets—and of course, a simple bowl of fresh berries at breakfast. ¶ In the garden, the leaves on each 5- to 6-foot shrub emerge in the spring in deep bronze shades lightening to pale green. Over the summer, they darken to deep green before turning red or yellow in fall. If there is room in your fruit garden, separate them into beds, growing at least two of each variety spaced 3 feet apart to ensure a harvest of early, mid-season, and late-season berries. Because the blueberry is such a well-behaved shrub, in a smaller garden they can be incorporated into flower beds or borders or used as a hedge. Related to rhododendrons, they prefer the same growing conditions of moist, acid soil, so work in lots of acid-balanced compost and nitrogen before planting, and thickly mulch with sawdust, pine needles, or well-rotted leaves. ¶ **HOW TO DO IT** ¶ In early spring, purchase your bare-root berry bushes. Keep the roots damp if you cannot plant the bushes immediately. Before planting, remove the wrappings and submerge the roots in a deep sink or bucket of water for 4 to 6 hours. Check the root ball, pruning back any broken or overly long roots. Prepare the soil by digging in quantities of organic compost to create a loose soil that holds moisture. ¶ Dig a hole in a sunny location just big enough to fit in the root mass with the top of the root ball at soil level. Make a pyramid of soil in the middle of the hole, spreading the roots over it. Add soil around the sides, tamping down as you go, continuing to add soil until it reaches the top of the roots. Water again thoroughly, and add more soil if the level ✓

Blueberry
Vaccinium species

What You Need
6 blueberry plants
15 feet of planting bed
Organic compost
All-purpose slow-release fertilizer granules
Acid-type mulch, such as pine needles,
sawdust, or well-rotted leaves

Pollination Requirements
2 varieties for best pollination

Light Conditions
4 to 6 hours or more of full sun

Growth Pattern
Shrublike bush

Pruning
Keep center of bush open; prune out
4-year-old canes; pinch back tips
after fruiting

Fruit Thinning
Unnecessary

Hardiness
Hardy to -25°F

Chill Requirement
700 to 800 hours

drops. Space plants 3 feet apart in beds with 3 feet between each row. Mulch the top of the soil near the crown with 3 to 5 inches of acidic material such as pine needles, sawdust, or wood bark. ¶ Water the new plants near the root crown every day for 5 days, then water consistently to keep the soil moist but not soggy. The following fall, scatter slow-release fertilizer granules over the bed according to the manufacturer's instructions. Renew the mulch every fall.

CURRANTS

Currants come in colors of white, red, and black, but the white is just a variety of the red, so the two varieties are Ribes nigrum and r. rubrum. Black currants are widely used as folk medicines, which science has verified by finding them high in vitamin C. ¶ Currants have been outlawed in the past because they foster the white blister rust that is such a serious problem to white pine trees. Both plants must be present for the fungus to complete its cycle. Consequently, currants should not be planted within 1,500 feet of such trees, unless they are the newly introduced disease-resistant currants. If a potential problem exists, gardeners should check with their agricultural extension agent before planting. ¶ For most gardeners, however, blister rust is not a problem, and currants can be introduced into the garden. The deciduous bushes grow up to be 3- to 5-foot-tall hedges, the berries following the flowers thickly clustered on stems. The little tassels at the end of the berries are the remnants of the flowers. Fruit on older canes are borne on stubby fruit spurs growing off the main cane, so be sure not to prune them. The fruits ripen in early summer, summoning hosts of birds to share the harvest. Row covers can defeat these feathered connoisseurs. ¶ Old-fashioned garden books talk of espaliered currants as well as bushes shaped into pyramids. For bushes in beds or hedges, simply prune out older branches, encouraging 1-, 2-, and 3-year-old stems, which fruit heavily. ¶ Black currant leaves make a highly esteemed herbal tea, and the berries may be cooked into jam or syrup, made into wine, or brewed into the famous French cordial, cassis, which added to white wine makes the drink Kir. Red and white currants are used similarly, and are often added to raspberries to provide a tart note in raspberry jam. ¶ **HOW TO DO IT** ¶ In early spring, purchase your bare-root currant bushes. Keep the roots damp if you cannot plant the bushes immediately. Before planting, remove the wrappings and submerge the roots in a deep sink or bucket of water for 4 to 6 hours. Check the root ball, pruning back any broken ✒

Black Currant
Ribes nigrum
❧

Red and White Currant
Ribes rubrum
❧

What You Need
5 bare-root currant plants • 20 feet of planting bed • Organic compost • All-purpose slow-release organic fertilizer granules
❧

Pollination Requirements
Self-fertile
❧

Light Conditions
4 to 6 hours or more of full sun; partial shade in hot summer areas
❧

Growth Pattern
Stems with fruit borne at bottom first year, then on spurs of second- and third-year stems
❧

Pruning
Prune out third-year canes at end of season
❧

Fruit Thinning
Unnecessary
❧

Hardiness
Hardy to -25°F
❧

Chill Requirement
800 hours
❧

or overly long roots. ¶ Dig a hole in a sunny location just big enough to fit in the root mass with the top of the root ball at soil level. Make a pyramid of soil in the middle of the hole, spreading the roots over it. Add soil around the sides, tamping down as you go, continuing to add soil until it reaches the top of the roots. Water again thoroughly, and add more soil if the level drops. Space plants 4 feet apart in beds with 3 feet between each row. Mulch the top of the soil near the crown with 3 inches of organic compost. ¶ Water the new plants near the root crown every day for 5 days, then water 12 inches out from the crowns once a week, or as needed to keep the soil moist but not soggy. The following fall, scatter slow-release fertilizer granules over the bed according to the manufacturer's instructions. Renew the mulch every fall.

POMEGRANATES

Cutting open a pomegranate reveals shimmering little rubies arranged in starlike enclosures between bitter yellow membranes. ¶ An ancient fruit said to have been developed by the Carthaginians, the pomegranate plant has a long history. The bark was used to make a tonic, the rind was a source of ink, and the juice was turned into grenadine. The juice has also been used in marinades. ¶ Pomegranates like long hot summers and full days of sun. In cooler summer areas, they will show off their red flowers in spring but will not set fruit. To increase heat, grow them against a west-facing wall and cover the ground with black plastic. The flowers give way to pinky-red fruits that grow to softball size. The shrub grows to 12 feet tall, and because it grows a dense cover in spring, it makes a handsome hedge. ¶ Prune to open up the shrub to light, cutting out crossing branches and any older wood. Cut out suckers at the base, and thin multiple stems to 2 or 3 at the most. ¶ **HOW TO DO IT** ¶ Submerge the pomegranate in its container in a deep sink or bucket of water until the air stops bubbling out of the container. Dig a hole in a sunny location just big enough to fit in the root mass with the top of the root ball at soil level. Add soil around the sides, tamping down as you go, continuing to add soil until it reaches the top of the roots. Water again thoroughly, and add more soil if the level drops. Mulch the top of the soil with 3 inches of organic compost, but pull the compost back 2 inches from the trunk. ¶ Water the shrub near the trunk every day for 5 days, then water consistently 12 to 24 inches out from the trunk to keep the soil moist but not soggy. The following fall, dig in slow-release fertilizer granules in a circle 24 inches out from the trunk according to the manufacturer's instructions. Renew the mulch every year.

Pomegranate
Punica granatum

❧

What You Need
Pomegranate in gallon can
Organic compost
All-purpose slow-release organic fertilizer granules

❧

Pollination Requirements
Self-fruitful

❧

Light Conditions
8 hours of full sun

❧

Growth Pattern
Shrub

❧

Pruning
Prune out old, dead, or diseased wood; open interior to sun; cut suckers back to 2 or 3 major stems

❧

Fruit Thinning
Unnecessary

❧

Hardiness
Hardy to 12°F

❧

Chill Requirement
100 to 200 hours

❧

FRUIT
TREES

What gardener doesn't long to have a garden graced with the off-kilter lines and spreading hoary limbs of an ancient apple tree? But, not every gar-

den has room for a 25-foot-wide tree, and when a gardener has to choose between one large tree versus generous beds of perennials, the choice goes to the greater diversity. ❧ Yet, determined gardeners can carve out space for fruit trees in the smallest of gardens, either in the ground or in containers. Finding room for trees is a matter of revisualizing the space and the ability of the trees to fit the space. Don't be tied to a vision of fruit trees in neat orchard rows. ❧ Look for a convenient fence or wall to espalier a dwarf or mid-size fruit tree. If you have room for just one tree and your fruit choice needs a pollinator, consider either planting two trees in one hole or choosing a tree grafted with three to five different types of fruit vari- eties. Choose self-fertile varieties that don't need another tree for pollination. ❧ Consider genetically dwarf fruit trees, which grow 8 to 10 feet tall and are just right for a border hedge or as a single tree punctuating a perennial border. A non-bearing hedge can be replaced with fruit trees chosen to fit the space and pruned to stay within bounds. Group three trees in an awkward corner or train trees over an arbor. Transform a small sunny side yard into a city orchard. ❧ Don't forget that you can plant under fruit trees. Under planting can add interest by contrasting with the color of the blooms or the fruit, and the soil will benefit from the protection from the sun, much like mulching. Particularly elegant are drifts of early-blooming spring bulbs that soak up the sunshine before the tree leafs out. ❧ Of course, matching the climate of your garden to the variety of fruit tree remains of paramount importance for successful fruit production. Remember that different types of trees have different requirements. Deciduous fruit trees need chilling hours, but some kinds require fewer than others, and within varieties, cultivars themselves will differ in their needs. Consult with local experts for types that are sure to succeed in your garden.

Fabulous Apricot

Apricots are thought to have originated in China. However, Alexander the Great found them in Armenia and assumed this to be their origin, accounting for their Latin name. The small tree is self-pollinating and long-lived, with a graceful, wide canopy. ¶ Because they are among the earliest blooming of the fruit trees, the buds of the apricot are susceptible to late frosts. If frost is a problem, site the tree in a northern or western exposure protected from morning sunlight. If the buds have a chance to thaw before direct sunlight hits them, frost damage may be minimized. ¶ Fruiting spurs bear for 4 years, so prune new wood less radically. The trees are susceptible to blights and brown rot disease. Prune the tree to be open in the center and destroy any diseased fruit. ¶ **HOW TO DO IT** ¶ In early spring, purchase your bare-root apricot tree. Keep the roots damp if you cannot plant the tree immediately. Before planting, remove the wrapping and submerge the roots in a deep sink or bucket of water for 4 to 6 hours. Check the root ball, pruning back any broken or overly long roots. ¶ Dig a hole in a sunny location just big enough to fit in the root mass with the top of the root ball at soil level. Make a pyramid of soil in the middle of the hole, spreading the roots over it. Add soil around the sides, tamping down as you go, continuing to add soil until it reaches the top of the roots. Water again thoroughly, and add more soil if the level drops. Mulch the top of the soil with 3 inches of organic compost, but pull the compost back 2 inches from the trunk. ¶ Water the tree near the trunk every day for 5 days, then water consistently 12 to 24 inches out from the trunk to keep the soil moist but not soggy. The following fall, dig in slow-release fertilizer granules in a circle 24 inches out from the trunk according to the manufacturer's instructions. Renew the mulch every year.

Apricot
Prunus Armeniaca: 'Moorpark',
'Blenheim'

What You Need
Bare-root apricot tree
Organic compost
All-purpose slow-release organic
fertilizer granules

Pollination Requirements
Self-fertile

Light Conditions
4 to 6 hours or more of full sun

Growth Pattern
Spur

Pruning
Prune to open center or modified open center; prune lightly to avoid cutting
off fruit spurs

Fruit Thinning
Thin fruits after early summer drop

Hardiness
Hardy

Chill Requirement
500 to 700 hours

Genetic dwarf peach tree

Genetically dwarf trees are small by nature, but they are also grafted onto rootstock that diminishes them and adds other good traits to their growth habit. You may see them written up in catalogues as "miniature" or "tiny" trees. ¶ Don't think that because the tree is small, the fruit or the harvest will be small, for that is not the case. ¶ Peaches are heavy feeders and like moist soil. They bear on new wood, so prune vigorously every spring for a good harvest. Use the open-center pruning style to ensure plenty of light and air in the center of the tree. ¶ **HOW TO DO IT** ¶ In early spring, purchase your bare-root grafted dwarf peach tree. Keep the roots damp if you cannot plant it immediately. Before planting, remove the wrappings and submerge the roots in a deep sink or bucket of water for 4 to 6 hours. Check the root ball, pruning back any broken or overly long roots. ¶ Dig a hole in a sunny location just big enough to fit in the root mass with the top of the root ball at soil level. Make a pyramid of soil in the middle of the hole, spreading the roots over it. Add soil around the sides, tamping down as you go, continuing to add soil until it reaches the top of the roots. Water again thoroughly, and add more soil if the level drops. Mulch the top of the soil with 6 inches of organic compost, but pull the compost 2 inches back from the trunk. ¶ Water the tree near the trunk every day for 5 days, then water 12 to 24 inches out from the trunk every week or as needed to keep the soil moist but not soggy. The following fall, dig in slow-release organic fertilizer granules in a circle 24 inches out from the trunk according to the manufacturer's instructions. Renew the mulch every year.

Genetic Dwarf Peach Tree
Prunus persica
❧

What You Need
Bare-root grafted genetic dwarf peach tree
Organic compost
All-purpose slow-release organic
fertilizer granules
❧

Pollination Requirements
Self-fertile
❧

Light Conditions
4 to 6 hours or more of full sun
❧

Growth Pattern
Spur
❧

Pruning
Prune to open center
❧

Fruit Thinning
Thin fruits after early summer drop
❧

Hardiness
Hardy to -15°F when established
❧

Chill Requirement
500 hours
❧

Two cherry trees in one planting hole

Garden book instructions call for spacing standard-sized trees at least 12 feet apart, but when space is at a premium you should consider planting two trees in one hole. This technique allows you to plant a pollinator when required, or to space out your harvest with two trees bearing successively. ¶ The cherry is the perfect fruit tree for this planting technique. One cherry, though it will bear profuse amounts of lovely flowers, cannot fruit unless one of another variety resides within 40 yards. Cherries are not self-fertile, so they require another variety for pollination. Planting two of the same cultivars in one hole will not result in fruit. ¶ Sweet cherries come in yellow Queen Anne or Rainier cherries or the red Bing type, which has rich dark flesh. Sour cherries are a different variety, not just unripe sweet cherries. Sometimes called pie cherries, these are self-fertile and can, depending what other cherry trees are in the vicinity, act as a pollinator. Grafted dwarf fruit trees grow about 15 feet in height instead of the standard 30 feet. Some of the newer grafted trees are self-fertile, in which case, you may want to plant one sweet and one sour cherry tree. Check the pollination requirements of your trees to assure cross-pollination and a good fruit set. ¶ Dig a hole large enough to hold both sets of roots. Set in the plants so each has space for the roots to spread. When the planting is complete, prune off the branches that cross from one tree into the other. As the trees mature, continue to prune off major crossing branches so that the two trees look like a double-trunked tree. ¶ **HOW TO DO IT** ¶ In early spring, purchase your bare-root cherry trees. Keep the roots damp if you cannot plant the trees immediately. Before planting, remove the wrappings and submerge the roots in a deep sink or bucket of water for 4 to 6 hours. Check the root balls, pruning back any broken or overly long roots. ¶ Dig a hole in a sunny location just big enough to fit the two root masses with the top of the root balls at soil level, probably about 2 to 3 feet in diameter. Make a pyramid of soil ✐

Sweet Cherry
Prunus Avium: 'Garden Bing', 'Stella', 'Rainier'
❧

Sour "Pie" Cherry
Prunus cerasus: 'Montmorency', 'Morello'
❧

What You Need
2 bare-root dwarf cherry trees
Organic compost
All-purpose slow-release fertilizer granules
❧

Pollination Requirements
Self-sterile cherries need another variety to pollinate
❧

Light Conditions
6 or more hours of full sun
❧

Growth Pattern
Spur
❧

Pruning
Prune to central leader and cut out crossing branches to create appearance of double-trunked tree
❧

Fruit Thinning
Unnecessary
❧

Hardiness
Hardy
❧

Chill Requirement
700 hours
❧

on one side of the hole, spreading the roots of one tree over it. Do the same for the other tree. Add soil around the sides of both root balls, tamping down as you go, continuing to add soil until it reaches the top of the roots. Water again thoroughly, and add more soil if the level drops. Mulch the top of the soil with 3 inches of organic compost, but pull the compost back 2 inches from the trunks. ¶ Water the trees near their trunks every day for 5 days, then water 12 to 24 inches out from the trunk weekly, or as needed to keep the soil moist but not soggy. The following fall, dig in slow-release organic fertilizer granules in a circle 24 inches out from the trunk according to the manufacturer's instructions. Renew the mulch every year.

ESPALIER FRUIT

We can be thankful to the gardener who first thought of shaping a tree flat against a wall, thereby increasing the warmth available to the tree, nurturing heat-loving fruits so they sweeten to the utmost. ¶ To start your apprenticeship, try the T-shape, a simple form that prunes the tree flat against a wall or fence to which are attached 3 horizontal training wires spaced 18 inches apart. Prepare to be patient for about 6 years to receive the full effect of the form, although you will taste fruit before that time. ¶ Use a dwarf fruit tree, for its size and vigor will make a showy espalier. Summer pruning will help to restore the form while restricting vigorous suckering. ¶ **HOW TO DO IT** ¶ In early spring, purchase your bare-root fruit tree. Keep the roots damp if you cannot plant it immediately. Before planting, remove the wrappings and submerge the roots in a deep sink or bucket of water for 4 to 6 hours. Check the root ball, pruning back any broken or overly long roots. Dig a hole 8 inches away from a fence or wall in a sunny location just big enough to fit in the root mass with the top of the root ball at soil level. Make a pyramid of soil in the middle of the hole, spreading the roots over it. Add soil around the sides, tamping down as you go, continuing to add soil until it reaches the top of the roots. Water again thoroughly, and add more soil if the level drops. Mulch the top of the soil with 3 inches of organic compost, but pull the compost 2 inches back from the trunk. Water the tree near the trunk every day for 5 days, then water 12 to 24 inches out from the trunk weekly, or as needed to keep the soil moist but not soggy. The following fall dig in slow-release fertilizer granules in a circle 24 inches out from the trunk according to the manufacturer's instructions. Renew the mulch every year. ¶ To create the espalier, the first winter, prune the leader just below the lowest wire. ✤

Dwarf Pear, Apricot, Apple, or Quince
Pyrus communis; Prunus armeniaca; Amalus; Cydonia oblonga

❧

What You Need
Bare-root dwarf fruit tree
Organic compost
All-purpose slow-release organic fertilizer granules

❧

Pollination Requirements
Depends on variety

❧

Light Conditions
4 to 6 hours or more of full sun

❧

Growth Pattern
Depends upon variety

❧

Pruning
Prune in winter to shape plant to 3 horizontal wires; summer prune to pinch back vigorous growth, balancing growth on one side of the tree with the other

❧

Fruit Thinning
Depends on variety

❧

Hardiness
Hardy

❧

Chill Requirement
Depends on variety

❧

Let 3 shoots grow up. Train the center one vertically and spread the other two horizontally along the wires, tying them loosely so as not to force the branches too severely. The second winter, top the central leader just below the second wire and cut back the two horizontal branches on the lower wire to 18 inches long. The third winter, top the leader below the third wire, and prune back the bottom laterals to 36 inches and the middle laterals to 18 inches. In the following years, prune off any shoots from the central leader in summer pruning, and in the winter prune back the horizontal arms. ¶ In the first years, don't prune shoots on the trunk, but allow them to grow to shade the trunk to protect it from sunscald.

HEIRLOOM

AND EXOTIC

VARIETIES

Trips to other continents reveal to gardeners how many superb varieties of fruit exist that are never seen on the supermarket shelves in the United States. In many cases, even if they are grown here, these fruits are too perishable for commercial travel, or they succeed only in a circumscribed area of climate. Sometimes, they need careful cosseting because, although their flavors excel, they may not have been bred for disease resistance or increased yield. Many varieties, picked ripe, are so perishable they last only two or three days. ❧ Commercial growers reject fruits for these shortcomings, but home gardeners ignore such reasoning. Oftentimes, what an orchardist considers a minuscule harvest represents an overwhelming bounty to a home grower. And when the major transportation is from the backyard directly to the kitchen, fragility seems unimportant. Disease resistance can be more of a problem, but when it is a question of nursing just one or two trees, again the problem diminishes. ❧ Heirloom or exotic fruits deliver flavor, color, texture, and taste. Varieties that were once revered became extinct as the commercial fruit producers rejected them for their eccentricities. Just as plant explorers once traveled to exotic places, plant preservationists now search deserted farm orchards, journey to historic districts, and even scout old cemeteries for the scion stock of ancient varieties thought to be lost. Today, you can plant fruit varieties that were spread across Europe by the Roman army, or taste a variety that was raved about by European monarchs, depicted by master painters, celebrated in poetry. ❧ Although nursery aisles may not carry these more unusual types, mail-order catalogues, arboretums, botanical gardens, and exotic fruit societies have enough variety to astonish most gardeners.

Antique apples

The ancient Romans described their feasts as proceeding not "from soup to nuts," but "ab ovo usque ad mala," for they traditionally started their full-course meals with eggs and ended them with apples, one of their favorite fruits. ¶ You may have to search out the older varieties in specialty catalogues, heirloom plant associations, or botanical gardens. They are well worth the effort, rewarding the grower with beautiful, highly flavored apples that are rarely, if ever, found in the marketplace. ¶ Apples must have a pollinator.

¶ **HOW TO DO IT** ¶ In early spring, purchase your bare-root grafted dwarf apple tree. Keep the roots damp if you cannot plant it immediately. Before planting, remove the wrapping and submerge the roots in a deep sink or bucket of water for 4 to 6 hours. Check the root ball, pruning back any broken or overly long roots. ¶ Dig a hole in a sunny location just big enough to fit in the root mass with the top of the root ball at soil level. Make a pyramid of soil in the middle of the hole, spreading the roots over it. Add soil around the sides, tamping down as you go, continuing to add soil until it reaches the top of the roots. Water again thoroughly, and add more soil if the level drops. Mulch the top of the soil with 3 inches of organic compost, but pull the compost back 2 inches from the trunk. ¶ Water the tree near the trunk every day for 5 days, then water 12 to 24 inches out from the trunk weekly or as needed to keep the soil moist but not soggy. The following fall, dig in slow-release organic fertilizer granules in a circle 24 inches out from the trunk according to the manufacturer's instructions. Renew the mulch every year.

Antique Apple
Malus pumila: 'Pink Pearl',
'Spitzenburg', 'White Winter Pearmain'

❧

What You Need
Bare-root apple tree
Organic compost
All-purpose slow-release organic
fertilizer granules

❧

Pollination Requirements
Self-sterile

❧

Light Conditions
4 to 6 hours or more of full sun

❧

Growth Pattern
Spur

❧

Pruning
Prune to central leader or
modified central leader

❧

Fruit Thinning
Thin fruits after early summer drop

❧

Hardiness
Hardy to -30°F, depending on variety

❧

Chill Requirement
600 to 800 hours, with exceptions

❧

Seckel Pear

The small rusty brown pear known as the Seckel may seem a dull choice compared with the plump pears that shine so brightly on the supermarket shelves. Yet the Seckel, bred in the second part of the nineteenth century, is consistently chosen as one of the best all-around pears by professional growers for its taste, texture, and ease of cultivation. A dainty 15- to 20-foot tree with an iron constitution, the Seckel resists fire blight, ignores bad weather and poor soil, and dutifully sets a huge crop of small but fragrantly delicious pears year after year. Self-fertile, the Seckel will fruit without another tree; the yield will be higher in the vicinity of another variety, although the Bartlett is not one of them. ¶ An ancient fruit, the charred remains of pears were found in the archeological sites of prehistoric European civilizations. They were well known to the Assyrians by 1000 B.C., and the Phoenicians, Greeks, and Romans all grew them. Cato described some six distinct types, Pliny forty-one, and Palladious fifty-six. At the turn of the eighteenth century, European breeders bred flavor and texture into the modern pear. ¶ Pears are one of the few fruits that must ripen off the tree. They must be picked only when the stem snaps off when the pear is gently twisted, otherwise the fruit will not develop its full flavor. Store home-picked pears wrapped in newspaper in a cool, dark place, checking after a week or 10 days to see if the color has changed and the telltale ripe fragrance is present. The ripe fruit will give slightly to pressure at the stem end. If you are in a hurry, store the fruit in a brown paper bag with a banana or apple, for the ethylene gas those fruits emit hurries the ripening of the pear. ¶ Seckels can be preserved as canned fruits; cooked into a sauce, pear butter, or chutney; made into cakes and pies; and of course, eaten fresh with blue cheese, toasted walnuts, and port. ¶ **HOW TO DO IT** ¶ In early spring, purchase your bare-root Seckel tree. Keep the roots damp if you cannot plant it immediately. Before planting, remove the wrappings and submerge the roots in a deep sink or bucket of water for 4 to 6 hours. Check the ✧

Seckel Pear
Pyrus communis

What You Need
Bare-root Seckel pear tree
Organic compost
All-purpose slow-release organic fertilizer granules

Pollination Requirements
Self-fertile, but crop increases with another pollinator

Light Conditions
4 to 6 hours or more of full sun

Growth Pattern
Spur

Pruning
Prune to central leader or modified open center

Fruit Thinning
Thin fruits after early-summer drop

Hardiness
Hardy to -2°F

Chill Requirement
600 hours

root ball, pruning back any broken or overly long roots. ¶ Dig a hole in a sunny location just big enough to fit in the root mass with the top of the root ball at soil level. Make a pyramid of soil in the middle of the hole, spreading the roots over it. Add soil around the sides, tamping down as you go, continuing to add soil until it reaches the top of the roots. Water again thoroughly, and add more soil if the level drops. Mulch the top of the soil with 3 inches of organic compost, but pull the compost back 2 inches from the trunk. ¶ Water the tree near the trunk every day for 5 days. Then water consistently 12 to 24 inches out from the trunk as needed to keep the soil moist but not soggy. The following fall, dig in slow-release organic fertilizer granules in a circle 24 inches out from the trunk according to the manufacturer's instructions. Renew the mulch every year.

SATSUMA PLUM

The satsuma was imported from Japan by Luther Burbank, who introduced it to the American public. ¶ Unlike many of the green- or golden-fleshed plums, the satsuma has a deep wine-red flesh and is partially freestone. The compact trees need only minimal pruning to keep them to a height of 20 feet. The plums grow so thickly from the short, stubby fruit spurs that thinning for larger fruits is advisable. Jams, chutneys, cakes, and put-by jars are particularly successful, for the rich taste of this plum holds up to cooking and the flesh doesn't turn mushy. ¶ **HOW TO DO IT** ¶ In early spring, purchase your bare-root satsuma tree. Keep the roots damp if you cannot plant it immediately. Before planting, remove the wrappings and submerge the roots in a deep sink or bucket of water for 4 to 6 hours. Check the root ball, pruning back any broken or overly long roots. ¶ Dig a hole in a sunny location just big enough to fit in the root mass with the top of the root ball at soil level. Make a pyramid of soil in the middle of the hole, spreading the roots over it. Add soil around the sides, tamping down as you go, continuing to add soil until it reaches the top of the roots. Water again thoroughly, and add more soil if the level drops. Mulch the top of the soil with 3 inches of organic compost, but pull the compost back 2 inches from the trunk. ¶ Water the tree near the trunk every day for 5 days, then water 12 to 24 inches out from the trunk weekly, or as needed to keep the soil moist but not soggy. After the tree has become established, it can take some drought. The following fall, dig in slow-release fertilizer granules in a circle 24 inches out from the trunk according to the manufacturer's instructions. Renew the mulch every year.

Satsuma Plum
Prunus salicina
❧

What You Need
Bare-root satsuma tree
Organic compost
All-purpose slow-release fertilizer granules
❧

Pollination Requirements
Pollinator necessary
❧

Light Conditions
4 to 6 hours or more of full sun
❧

Growth Pattern
Spur
❧

Pruning
Prune to open center; use thinning cuts
to keep tree open yet compact to
offset rapid early growth
❧

Fruit Thinning
Thin fruits after early summer drop
❧

Hardiness
Hardy
❧

Chill Requirement
300 to 500 hours
❧

OLD-FASHIONED QUINCE

Despite its bumpy, lumpy, yellowish appearance, the quince is an ancient fruit highly esteemed by the Persians, Egyptians, and Romans. The deciduous tree grows from 10 to 25 feet. In spring, its contorted, knobby form is clothed in huge white or pink blossoms. The fruit, when picked, radiates an exquisite flowery fragrance that perfumes whole rooms. It cannot be eaten raw; its flesh is almost rock hard and astringent, yet when cooked slowly, the acerbic flesh softens, blushes pink, and becomes meltingly tender. When the ripe fruit is baked or used in preserves, its fragrance permeates the dish. ¶ Harvest quince before the first frost when the color changes to deep yellow. Do not store with apples or pears, for the quince will take on their fragrance, losing its own. ¶ **HOW TO DO IT** ¶ In early spring, purchase your bare-root grafted quince tree. Keep the roots damp if you cannot plant it immediately. Before planting, remove the wrappings and submerge the roots in a deep sink or bucket of water for 4 to 6 hours. Check the root ball, pruning back any broken or overly long roots. ¶ Dig a hole in a sunny location just big enough to fit in the root mass with the top of the root ball at soil level. Make a pyramid of soil in the middle of the hole, spreading the roots over it. Add soil around the sides, tamping down as you go, continuing to add soil until it reaches the top of the roots. Water again thoroughly, and add more soil if the level drops. Mulch the top of the soil with 3 inches of organic compost, but pull the compost back 2 inches from the trunk. ¶ Water the tree near the trunk every day for 5 days, then water 12 to 24 inches out from the trunk weekly, or as needed to keep the soil moist but not soggy. The following fall, dig in slow-release fertilizer granules in a circle 24 inches out from the trunk according to the manufacturer's instructions. Renew the mulch every year.

Quince
Cydonia vulgaris:'Orange',
'Pineapple', 'Van Damen'

What You Need
Bare-root grafted quince tree
Organic compost
All-purpose slow-release fertilizer granules

Pollination Requirements
Self-fertile

Light Conditions
4 to 6 hours or more of full sun

Growth Pattern
Spur

Pruning
Prune to central leader or
modified central leader

Fruit Thinning
Thin fruits after early-summer drop

Hardiness
Hardy

Chill Requirement
250 to 300 hours

MULBERRIES

One of the oldest cultivated fruits, mulberries excel as an edible landscape plant. Yet a standard mulberry tree is not for the fainthearted, for most grow larger than a small garden can hold, topping off at 24 to 30 feet—and some types grow to 80. 'Black Beauty', a semi-dwarf variety, grows to 15 feet, however, and even a full-size tree can be stunted by pruning the main stem to produce multiple trunks. Expect the most popular 'Black Persian' and 'Illinois Everbearing' to grow to 45 feet. The ripe fruits will not keep even one day after being picked, although they freeze superbly. Fallen berries do make a mess, so don't plant a tree bordering a driveway, pathway, or terrace. ¶ The fruit may be fermented to make mulberry wine, cooked in pies, or made into syrup. ¶ **HOW TO DO IT** ¶ In early spring, purchase your bare-root grafted mulberry tree. Keep the roots damp if you cannot plant it immediately. Before planting, remove the wrappings and submerge the roots in a deep sink or bucket of water for 4 to 6 hours. Check the root ball, pruning back any broken or overly long roots. ¶ Dig a hole in a sunny location just big enough to fit in the root mass with the top of the root ball at soil level. Make a pyramid of soil in the middle of the hole, spreading the roots over it. Add soil around the sides, tamping down as you go, continuing to add soil until it reaches the top of the roots. Water again thoroughly, and add more soil if the level drops. Mulch the top of the soil with 3 inches of organic compost, but pull the compost back 2 inches from the trunk. ¶ Water the tree near the trunk every day for 5 days, then water consistently 12 to 24 inches out from the trunk to keep the soil moist but not soggy. The following fall, dig in slow-release organic fertilizer granules in a circle 24 inches out from the trunk according to the manufacturer's instructions. Renew the mulch every year.

Mulberry
Morus nigra: 'Black Beauty',
'Black Persian', 'Illinois Everbearing'
❧

What You Need
Bare-root grafted mulberry tree
Organic compost
All-purpose slow-release organic
fertilizer granules
❧

Pollination Requirements
Self-fertile
❧

Light Conditions
4 hours or more of full sun; can take
shade in hot summer climates
❧

Growth Pattern
single or multiple-trunked trees
❧

Pruning
Light thinning; prune to multiple trunks
if preferred to central leader
❧

Fruit Thinning
Unnecessary
❧

Hardiness
Hardy
❧

Chill Requirement
400 hours
❧

INTO THE
KITCHEN

Eating fruit out of hand, fresh off the bush, vine, or tree, has a great advantage: The intense sun-warmed flavor can hardly be bettered. Yet the bounty always overwhelms  the gardener, and an entire category of cooking has been developed to deal with the astonishing fertility of fruit plants. A kitchen filled with the fragrance of cooking fruit is only one of the rewards of growing your own. ❧ As the fruit grows in your garden, watch carefully to make sure it comes to perfect ripeness before it is picked. Color is a prime indicator: Blackberries go from red to deep blue black, strawberries grow bright red, peaches become a rich orange blushed with red. If a tree canopy is too full, however, apples and oranges may not color even though ripe. When fruit is ready to pick it separates easily from the tree. This holds true even for pears and Japanese persimmons, which ripen after picking. ❧ Process fruits as soon as possible after picking. Berries of all types should be washed just before using them. Drop berries into a bowl of cold water, give them a swirl, then drain them immediately in a colander. If using them much later, refrigerate with a sprinkle of sugar over the top. Otherwise, if you are serving them within 3 or 4 hours, let them sit at room temperature. ❧ Processing fruit in different forms allows you to sample summer's warmth and sweetness in midwinter. Grapes, apples, and pears can be dried, and most fruits can be canned, frozen, or made into jams, jelly, and syrups.

Fruit jams, vinegars, and syrups

The extravagant harvest of home-grown fruit is a luxury, but as with any riches, it is wise to store some away for a rainy day. Nothing could be easier than these recipes, and once you have tried them, you will see how quickly you can fill up your pantry with the abundance of summer. Preserves and syrups will keep under refrigeration for 3 to 4 months. To put up large quantities, cook in small batches and process in a boiling-water bath (see The Glass Pantry in the bibliography). ¶ **SUMMER FRUIT PRESERVES** ¶ This simple master recipe was given to me years ago and works for all fruits. For variety, a stick of cinnamon and some cloves add a hint of spice. Please note that homemade preserves will almost always be runnier than most commercial preserves. ¶ Makes ½ pint. ¶ **HOW TO DO IT** ¶ In a medium, heavy saucepan, combine all the ingredients and bring to a simmer over medium heat. Cook, stirring occasionally, for 30 minutes, or until a spoonful drops off in a sheet. Watch to see that the mixture doesn't burn, turning down the heat if it begins to stick to the bottom of the saucepan. Check the consistency by dropping a small amount onto a cold saucer. The drop should hold for a moment before breaking. Pour into hot sterilized jars, seal, and refrigerate for 3 to 4 months. ¶ Fruit syrup: Add 1 cup of water to the ingredients for the above recipe and cook the mixture for about 15 minutes, or until the syrup has thickened. Strain the cooked syrup, pour it in a hot sterilized bottle or jar, seal, and refrigerate for 3 to 4 months. Mix the syrup with sparkling water for a cooling drink; pour it over fresh fruit sorbet or ice cream for dessert; or use to top pancakes or French toast. Makes 1 pint. ¶ **FRUIT VINEGARS** ¶ *Fruit vinegars are well worth* ✒

Summer Fruit Preserves

❦

What You Need

1 cup fresh berries or sliced peeled fruit
1 cup sugar
1 lemon peel strip, 1 inch by 2 inches
1 cinnamon stick, optional
5 whole cloves, optional

❦

Fruit Vinegars

❦

What You Need

2 cups fresh whole berries or
sliced peeled fruit
About 2½ cups 5 percent cider vinegar,
distilled white vinegar, or red
or white wine vinegar
3 fresh basil or thyme sprigs, optional

❦

making because their piquant taste adds fine flavor to a variety of dishes such as salad dressings, sautés, and marinades. Fresh herbs add an intriguing flavor note. ¶ **HOW TO DO IT** ¶ Add the fruit to a hot sterilized 1-quart wide-mouthed canning jar. Pour enough vinegar over the fruit to completely fill the jar. If you are using herbs, add them now, making sure they are totally covered by the vinegar. Place the jar in a cool, dark place for 1 month, or until the vinegar tastes strongly of fruit. Strain out the fruit and pour the vinegar into a hot sterilized 250-ml bottle. Seal and store in a cool, dark place. The longer the vinegar ages, the smoother the taste.

CLAFOUTIS

Clafoutis, that French combination of sweet batter and fruit, is simple to make and lovely for either breakfast or dessert. ¶ *Serves 6 to 8* ¶ **HOW TO DO IT** ¶ Preheat the oven to 350°F. Butter an 8-cup baking dish or ovenproof casserole and arrange the fruit in the bottom. ¶ In a medium bowl, beat the eggs, milk, cream, brown sugar, and vanilla together until blended. In a small bowl, mix the salt, flour, cinnamon, and cardamom together. Add the dry ingredients to the wet ingredients and beat until smooth. Pour the batter over the fruit. ¶ Bake the clafoutis 30 to 35 minutes, or until it turns golden brown and a knife inserted in the center comes out clean. Sprinkle the lemon juice over the top and dust the clafoutis with confectioners' sugar. Serve warm.

What You Need

1 1/2 cups fresh berries or sliced pitted plums or apricots, sliced figs, or sliced peeled and pitted peaches
3 eggs
1 cup milk
1/4 cup heavy cream
1/4 cup packed brown sugar
1 tablespoon vanilla extract
1/4 teaspoon salt
2/3 cup all-purpose flour
1 tablespoon ground cinnamon
1/4 teaspoon ground cardamom
2 tablespoons fresh lemon juice
Confectioners' sugar for dusting

OLD-FASHIONED UPSIDE-DOWN CAKE WITH FRESH FRUIT

Upside-down cake, the homely American dessert made with canned pineapple rings and maraschino cherries, is a different creature altogether when made with home-grown fresh fruit. ¶ *Serves 8* ¶ **HOW TO DO IT** ¶ Preheat the oven to 350°F. To make the topping: In a small saucepan, melt the butter and brown sugar together over low heat, stirring constantly until the sugar is dissolved. Pour the butter mixture into a 12-inch springform pan, spreading it evenly with a rubber spatula. Distribute the fruit over the butter mixture and set aside. ¶ In a medium bowl, beat the butter and sugar together until smooth. Beat in the eggs and vanilla until smooth. In a small bowl, stir the flour, baking powder, and salt together. Alternately beat the dry ingredients and milk into the egg mixture by thirds to make a smooth batter. Add the vanilla and beat just until the mixture is smooth. Pour the batter over the fruit and spread it evenly with a rubber spatula. ¶ Bake for 30 to 40 minutes, or until a skewer inserted in the center comes out clean. Let cool in the pan for 2 minutes. Place a serving plate over the top of the cake and, holding it firmly, turn the cake upside down to reverse it onto a plate. Should any of the topping stick to the bottom of the pan, simply use a knife to remove it and add it to the top of the cake. Serve warm, on a pool of fruit syrup if you like, with whipped cream or vanilla ice cream.

What You Need
❧
Topping
4 tablespoons butter
1/4 cup packed dark brown sugar
❧
10 stone fruits, halved and pitted
1/3 cup (2/3 stick) butter
2/3 cup granulated sugar
2 eggs
1 teaspoon vanilla extract
1 1/3 cups all-purpose flour
2 teaspoons baking powder
1/2 teaspoon salt
2/3 cup milk
Fruit syrup (see page 98), optional
❧
Whipped cream or vanilla ice cream
for serving
❧

Fresh fruit cake topped with almond-streusel topping

Although this recipe, when I first came across it, specified peaches, with practice I discovered that any fresh stone fruit bakes up superbly, and apricots are fabulous. Although quite easy, the recipe looks complicated so it wows as a fancy dinner dessert. If you are short of time, leave off the almond-streusel topping and add a dollop of whipped cream or vanilla ice cream. ¶ **HOW TO DO IT** ¶ Preheat the oven to 350 °F. ¶ Butter a 12-inch springform pan. Space the apricot halves, cut side down, evenly inside the pan. Start around the sides, making circles of fruit until there is room only for one in the very center. ¶ In the bowl of a mixer or a food processor, add the melted butter, milk, egg, and vanilla. Mix together thoroughly for 1 minute. Then in a separate mixing bowl, mix together the flour, sugar, baking powder, and salt. Add the flour mixture to the creamed mixture, beating just until the mixture is smooth, about 2 minutes. Set aside. ¶ In a medium-size bowl, cream together the butter and the sugar. Mix in the almonds, flour, and cinnamon. Stir well to combine. ¶ Pour the cake batter over the fruit. With your fingers, break up and sprinkle the almond mixture in large crumbs over the surface of the cake. Place the cake in the oven and bake for 25 minutes, or until the top is golden brown and a knife inserted into the middle of the cake comes out clean. Dust the top with confectioners' sugar, and serve warm.

What You Need

10 apricots, halved and pitted, or any other stone fruit
⅓ cup butter, melted
1 cup milk
1 egg
1 teaspoon vanilla
1¼ cups all-purpose flour
1 cup sugar
2½ teaspoons baking powder
1 teaspoon salt
Whipped cream or ice cream, optional
Confectioners' sugar for dusting

Almond Topping

½ cup butter
½ cup sugar
1 cup coarsely ground unbleached almonds
2 tablespoons unbleached all-purpose flour
1 teaspoon cinnamon

Plant sources

Some nurseries ask for a refundable fee for their catalogue. When there is no phone number, send a self-addressed, stamped envelope with your request for a catalogue.

Abundant Life Seed
Foundation
P.O. Box 772
Port Townsend, WA 98368
206-385-5660,
fax 206 385-7455
Offers 11 different types of berries.

Ahrens Strawberry Nursery
Route 1
Huntington, IN 47542
101 different berries.

Alliance Nursery
5965 Alliance Road
Marianna, FL 32448
904-762-3761
*Fruit trees for the southeast;
88 different berries.*

Chestnut Hill Nursery
Route 1, P.O. Box 341
Alachua, FL 32615
800-669-2067,
fax 904-462-4330
*Kaki persimmons, figs, cold-hardy
citrus, mulberries, and low-chill
fruit trees.*

Edible Landscaping
Michael McConkey
P.O. Box 77
Afton, VA 22920
804-361-9134
38 different low-care fruit varieties.

Henry Field Seed & Nursery
415 N. Burnett Street
Shenandoah, IA 51602
74 fruits and 63 berries.

Northwoods Retail Nursery
27635 S. Oglesby Road
Canby, OR 97013
503-266-5432
*116 fruits and 74 berries;
specializes in resistant stock.*

Peaceful Valley Farm Supply
P.O. Box 2209
Grass Valley, CA 95945
916-272-4769
*Natural pest management and
organic fertilizers.*

Sonoma Antique Apple
Nursery
4395 Westside Road
Healdsburg, CA 95448
707-542-5510
*Specializes in heritage fruits;
offers over 200 varieties.*

Stark Brothers Nursery
Hwy. 54, P.O. Box 10
Louisiana, MO 63353
800-325-4180,
fax 314-754-5290
*Only U.S. source of apple
collonades, plus 171 other fruits.*

Bibliography

Bailey, L. H.
*The Standard Cyclopedia of
Horticulture.*
New York: Macmillan, 1950.

Barry, P.
Barry's Fruit Garden.
New York: Orange Judd
Company, 1909.

Brennan, Georgeanne
The Glass Pantry.
San Francisco:
Chronicle Books, 1994.

Brickell, Christopher.
*Pruning: A Step-by-Step Guide to
Pruning Roses, Deciduous Shrubs,
Evergreens, Hedges, Wall Shrubs,
Fruit Bushes & Trees, and
Deciduous Trees.*
New York: Simon &
Schuster, 1988.

Flowerdew, Bob.
The Complete Book of Fruit.
New York: Penguin Studio,
1995.

Hobhouse, Penelope.
*Penelope Hobhouse's Gardening
Through the Ages.*
New York: Simon &
Schuster, 1992.

Hortus Third Dictionary.
New York: Macmillan, 1976.

Jellicoe, Geoffrey and Susan;
Goode, Patrick;
Lancaster, Michael.
Oxford Companion to Gardens.
New York: Oxford
University Press, 1991.

Kourik, Robert.
*Designing and Maintaining Your
Edible Landscape Naturally.*
Santa Rosa: Metamorphic
Press, 1986.

Sunset Western Garden Book.
Menlo Park: Sunset
Publishing Corporation,
1995.

Whealy, Kent, and
Demuth, Steve, eds.
*Fruit, Berry, and Nut Inventory:
An Inventory of Nursery Catalogs
Listing All Fruit, Berry, and Nut
Varieties Available by Mail Order
in the United States.*
Decorah, IA:
Seed Saver Publications,
1993.

Index

Acknowledgments

A book is much like a fruit garden, rich with flavors from many sources that help to make up the whole. At the Lescher Agency, Susan Lescher, Mickey Choate, and Carolyn Larson started the process, like selecting all the best varieties of fruit. At Chronicle Books, Leslie Jonath and Carole Goodman continued the work, like tilling the soil in preparation for planting. Carolyn Miller's copyediting helped to prune and shape the prose. The elegant design of Aufuldish & Warinner gave order and balance to the overall scheme. Faith was inspired and aided by her friends at The Apple Farm, Bob and Harolyn, Susan and Carrie, the Wags, Fred the kiwi king, Michelle and Maya, Sandra, Kelly, Joan and Jim, Virginia, David, and all her patient neighbors. Robert Kourik, a noted expert in the field, gave Mimi technical assistance and checked the manuscript; she also received help from Carolyn and Terry Hanson of the Sonoma Antique Nursery. Faith and Mimi, as always, had the kind support, like poles that hold up fruit-laden branches, of Bruce, and Daniel and Arann Harris.